CREATING
STORIES
THAT
CONNECT

CREATING
STORIES
A PASTOR'S GUIDE
TO STORYTELLING
THAT
CONNECT

D. BRUCE SEYMOUR

Kregel
Academic & Professional

Creating Stories That Connect: A Pastor's Guide to Storytelling

© 2007 by D. Bruce Seymour

Published by Kregel Publications, a division of Kregel, Inc., P.O. Box 2607, Grand Rapids, MI 49501.

Library of Congress Cataloging-in-Publication Data
Seymour, D. Bruce.
Creating stories that connect : a pastor's guide to storytelling / by D. Bruce Seymour.
    p. cm.
Includes bibliographical references and indexes.
    1. Storytelling—Religious aspects—Christianity.
2. Theology—Methodology. I. Title.
BT83.78.S495 2007
251—dc22   2007000186

ISBN 978-0-8254-3671-0

Printed in the United States of America

07 08 09 10 11 / 5 4 3 2 1

To my wife,
Connie,
who was the first to believe
I would write a book.

To my church family,
New Monmouth Baptist Church,
with deep gratitude for their generous support.

To the special friends who listened to my stories
as we walked dark valleys together.

Contents

Introduction 9

1. All About Stories. 15
2. Why We Use Stories 24
3. How to Put a Story Together 40
4. Special Ministry Stories. 49
5. How a Ministry Story Works 57
6. When a Story Is the Best Response. 68
7. Creating an Original Ministry Story 80
8. How to Encourage Stories 126

Bibliography 131
Title Index. 135
Topical Index. 137

Introduction

We live in story like fish in the sea.
—JOHN DOMINIC CROSSAN

LET ME TELL YOU A STORY. . . . When we hear those words, we feel a flutter of excitement, don't we? The words quicken a sense of anticipation and a swirl of questions: What happened? Who did it? Where? When? Why? The story might have the answers.

Stories surround us, and it is good that they do. We need stories the way a fish needs water. We live and move immersed in stories. Stories help us make sense of the world. Stories help us pass our understanding on to others. Stories shape us. In a sense, stories mark us as human. Milton Dawes, a research scientist, suggests that stories are so intrinsic to humanity that "one way to describe our species is that we constitute a *storytelling form of life.*"[1]

We capture the truly important things in our lives in stories, as James Peterson, an elementary school teacher, illustrates in the following story:

---

1. Milton Dawes, "Science, Religion and God: My Story," *ETC: A Review of General Semantics* 57, no. 2 (2000): 149. Emphasis added.

Nearly twenty-five years ago, when I was teaching second grade, an incident happened to me that I shall never forget. I was working in a newly founded private school called the White Pony in suburban San Francisco. We only had four teachers working with kindergarten through third grade, and we all, therefore, had to share in playground supervision. It was my turn that day, and as I was watching the kids, a tiny five-year-old kindergartener plopped into my lap and put her arms around my neck. "I wish you were my teacher," she chirped. "Oh, really? Why is that?" I responded. "Because you know everything," she replied very seriously. "Oh, I do? What do you mean?" "Oh," she said, "you know stories and songs!" In her five-year-old world, everything that made up her humanness was summed up in two words: *stories* and *songs*.[2]

That little girl sensed the importance of stories. Maybe the most important things for all of us are the stories we tell and the songs we sing.

Because this is a book about stories, I suppose I should start by clearing up one thing right away. Stories are not just for children. Children like them, but everyone else does too. When we meet friends, we tell stories. The books we read, the shows we watch—even the commercials on TV—tell stories. Stories are universal, and they're for everyone, not just children.

We communicate our experience with language, and when the language is used in a story, the meaning of the experience becomes obvious. Stories are actually a very sophisticated way to process and communicate information. In other words, stories are a very *adult* form of language. They may not be the most serious form of language, but they are an important form of language.

In this book, I want to show why stories are important, why they are so attractive, and what makes them an effective way to

---

2.   James Peterson, "Once Upon a Time," *Paths of Learning,* no. 14 (2002): 33.

use language. If you understand why stories are so powerful, I believe you will want to tell more stories. You will want to use them in your teaching, include them in your sermons, and slip them into your counseling. I also believe you'll discover that stories will make your teaching more effective, your preaching more memorable, and your counseling more convincing.

I believe that telling more stories can make us more like Jesus. That may sound "over the top," but think about it. Jesus told stories all the time. He taught with stories. He answered questions with stories. He even rebuked with stories. So when we tell stories, we emulate Jesus—and that's a good thing! My goal is to inspire you to tell more stories, *original* stories, just as Jesus did.

Your interest in this book may suggest that you're already a pretty competent storyteller. You probably have quite a bit of experience collecting and using stories created by others, but that is not exactly what Jesus did. As far as we can tell, Jesus *created* the stories he used. I believe that is a skill we can learn. We may never be as good at it as Jesus was, because he was the Master, but we can learn from him. When we do, we will find that our stories have a measure of the same sort of power and effectiveness. My desire is to help you become more than a story*teller*; I want to help you become a story*maker*, like Jesus.

In order to become storymakers, we need to take a close look at the art of story—the sort of close, technical look that an aspiring painter would give to an original Rembrandt. We want to notice every stroke, shade, and detail about stories. We want to understand how they are put together, what makes them powerful, and when to use them.

Oddly enough, that sort of technical examination is unusual. C. S. Lewis once marveled, "It is astonishing how little attention critics have paid to Story considered in itself."[3] In this book, we want to pay attention to Story, and learn all we can about stories, so that we can create some of our own.

---

3. C. S. Lewis, *Of Other Worlds* (New York: Harvest, 1966), 3.

Let me give you a picture of how we can do that. Imagine that this book is like an eight-day mountain-climbing adventure trip. Over those eight days, we will scale the mountain peak we have chosen and come back down. We'll make the climb in three stages. Stage one will require three days of hiking through the foothills to the base of the mountain. Stage two will get us up the mountain to the tree line, another two days of climbing. Stage three will take us up to the peak itself and back down—three mostly vertical days.

This book is planned in the same three stages as our imaginary mountaineering trip. We'll take the first three chapters to hike through the foothills of general information about story. In chapter 1, we will see what a story is and what it does. Chapter 2 explores the six basic reasons why people use stories and how Jesus and other leaders used stories. In chapter 3 we will navigate a technical section of the trail and look at all the parts of a story—characters, context, plot, and climax. It will be a technical discussion, but it is only one chapter, and when we get through it, we will be at the base of the mountain we want to climb. We will understand what a story is, how to put one together, and how to use it.

In stage two, the next two chapters, we will start up Parable Mountain, the peak we have chosen to conquer. In these chapters, we will focus on a particular type of story—a ministry story. Jesus told ministry stories that we call parables, so in chapter 4 we will take a close look at parables—where they came from and what makes them special. We will also look at other ministry stories, such as fables. Chapter 5 is another technical climb because we want to look at how parables work, how to put one together, and how to interpret them. When we finish this stage of the climb, we will be out of the trees and will have the summit clearly in view. We will have good understanding of stories in general, and ministry stories in particular. We will be ready to push to the peak—creating our own ministry stories.

In some ways, stage three will be the hardest part of the climb.

Very few people have tried to scale this particular peak—creating their own ministry stories—but with what we will learn in stages one and two, we will be in position to accomplish this goal. In chapter 6, we will come to understand when a story is the best response. We will look at when Jesus used ministry stories and when other leaders use stories. In chapter 7, we will focus on the how-tos of parable making. In this chapter, I will offer some specific guidance on how to create a ministry story, and twenty examples of parables I have created for my own ministry. With each of my examples, I will share the situation that provoked the parable and an analysis of how well it worked. By the end of this chapter, you should be on top of the mountain—able to create your own ministry stories.

Chapter 8 is sort of like coming back down (which is an important part of any mountain-climbing adventure). I will share some suggestions for how you can use what you have learned to create a storymaking environment in your own church or ministry.

Maybe you are thinking, *This sounds like fun, but I could never do it. I could never create an original story.* Let me share some encouragement from John Walsh, an experienced pastor and storyteller:

> Storytelling is a gift we all have. God has given you this gift, and it is superior to the storytelling ability given to any other earthly creature. I compare it to the gift of smell that God gave dogs. Some dogs have a keener sense of smell than others, but they all have it. The worst nose on a dog is still hundreds of times more sensitive than the best human nose.[4]

None of us will ever be as good at telling stories as Jesus was, but the worst storyteller will be more interesting than the best list maker or bullet-point presenter. With practice, you can become

---

4. John Walsh, *The Art of Storytelling: Easy Steps to Presenting an Unforgettable Story* (Chicago: Moody, 2003), 12.

proficient and even skillful at storytelling, and it is worth the effort. The ability to tell a good story is part of our ministerial craft. Our Master told stories, and we should uphold the standard he set. As we tell our stories, we will do as Jesus did—teaching, directing, and inspiring others. Let the journey begin!

CHAPTER ONE

All About Stories

The universe is made of stories, not atoms.
—MURIEL RUKEYSER

BECAUSE THIS IS A BOOK ABOUT STORIES, we ought to start with a clear definition of story. Unfortunately, that is harder to do than one might think. Asking a person to define story is like asking a fish to define water. We are so immersed in stories that we hardly notice them. Still, a thoughtful fish could provide some insight, and a scholarly fish might provide all the definition anyone would want. Fortunately, there are many thoughtful people and a wide variety of scholars who have studied story and can provide insight and definition.

A Story Is a Description

Basically, a story is a description of something that happened. The description is usually presented in sequence, with a beginning, middle, and end. Stories are shaped to make a point, which should help us understand what happened.

Of course, there are more technical ways of saying that. *The Oxford English Dictionary* offers a helpful definition: "A recital of events that have or are alleged to have happened; a series of events that are or might be narrated."[1] Lynne Tirrell, a professor of philosophy at the University of Massachusetts in Boston, emphasizes the shape of the story in her definition: "[A story is] a narrative with a certain very specific syntactic shape (beginning-middle-end or situation-transformation-situation) and with a subject matter which allows for or encourages the projection of human values upon this material."[2] These definitions help us see that a story is a description of an event presented in a shape that helps us understand what the event means. *Shape* and *sequence* are fundamental aspects of story.

Stories Shape Our Experiences into Meaning

We all instinctively use stories to make sense of life. You might say we *live* life in events, and we *make sense* of life in stories. Experiences come one after another, and as we reflect on what happened, we instinctively shape those episodes into life lessons. The events mean something, and we put that meaning into words, which become stories. Stories are how we shape the raw data of our experiences into understanding and meaning. Paul Borden writes, "Story, like breathing or thinking, is an intrinsic part of our existence. We daydream, plot, criticize, hope and visualize ambitions in story form. No one lives life deductively."[3]

That is part of why stories are so powerful. The stories we tell about what happened shape that experience and give it meaning. If we continue to tell the same story about what happened, we sustain a particular way of understanding that event. Kevin Bradt, a Jesuit scholar and preacher observes, "Story is not just an art form but an epistemology, a technique, or way of knowing the world."[4] Bradt illustrates this point in a colorful way:

1. *The Oxford English Dictionary,* 2d ed., s.v. "story."
2. Lynne Tirrell, "Storytelling and Moral Agency," *Journal of Aesthetics and Art Criticism* 48, no. 2 (1990): 115.
3. Paul Borden, "Is There Really One Big Idea in That Story?" in *The Big Idea of Biblical Preaching,* ed. Keith Willhite and Scott M. Gibson (Grand Rapids: Baker, 1998), 67.
4. Kevin M. Bradt, *Story as a Way of Knowing* (Kansas City, MO: Sheed & Ward, 1997), 3.

> When bushes burst into flame, [Moses] did not think
> to measure the angles of the branches or the intensity
> of the flame's heat but removed his shoes, listened,
> heard, and knew that he was on holy ground. When seas
> parted, [Miriam] did not calculate the pull of the planets
> on the tides; she broke into song and danced her way
> across starfish and seashell to the safety of dry land and
> deliverance.[5]

A story conveys more than the information or the knowledge
of an event. A story teaches the meaning of the event and provides
understanding and wisdom.

Story is so essential to thought that some have described the
brain as a "narrative device" that "runs on stories."[6] Jerome Bruner,
an educational psychologist, goes even further and makes a compelling case that humans are born with a "prelinguistic readiness"
to order experiences in the form of stories. Bruner believes this
impulse to shape experience is so basic that it explains how young
children learn to talk.

> Narrative structure is even inherent in the praxis of social
> interaction before it achieves linguistic expression. . . . It
> is a "push" to construct narrative that determines the or-
> der of priority in which grammatical forms are mastered
> by the young child.[7]

We begin life with the desire to make stories, probably because
our first experiences with knowledge are aural. Before we were
born, we were already hearing. In the gospel of Luke, we are told
that John the Baptist leaped for joy in his mother's womb when
he *heard* Mary's voice and realized his Savior was nearby (Luke

---

5. Ibid., xiii.
6. Martha Combs and John D. Beach, "Stories and Storytelling: Personalizing the
Social Studies," *The Reading Teacher* 47, no. 6 (1994): 464.
7. Jerome Bruner, *Acts of Meaning* (Cambridge, MA: Harvard, 1990), 77.

1:41, 44). Modern fetal research has confirmed that babies in the womb respond to sound. Newborns in the delivery room are able to distinguish the sound of their mother's voice from all the other sounds in the room. As infants, all of us initially relied on sound to orient us to the world until our eyes learned to track and follow sounds and make the visual-oral-aural associations.[8] In other words, knowledge of the world around us was first experienced as sound. As a result, knowledge that comes to us aurally enters our understanding at a very basic level. We may grow up to be visual learners, but in a sense, aural knowledge has seniority because it was the first way we experienced knowledge.

The primacy of aural learning gives stories an intrinsic power. Stories enter into our experience aurally. Even stories that we read silently are "reactivated" as we "hear" the words in our heads. Kevin Bradt, citing Walter Ong, reminds us,

> The written text, for all its permanence, means nothing, is not even a text, except in relation to the spoken word. For a text to be intelligible, to deliver its message, it must be reconverted into sound, directly or indirectly, either really in the external world or in the auditory imagination. All verbal expression, whether put into writing, print, or the computer, is ineluctably bound to sound forever.[9]

Stories "bound to sound forever" enter our experience just as our very first experiences did. That makes them powerful.

Because our first experiences with knowledge were aural/oral, any sort of verbal communication is more powerful than simple written communication. Verbal communication comes with a broader context. Whenever a story is told, the sound of the words occurs within a context that we often call *body language*: motions, volume, pacing, tone, and more. Even the situation that provoked the story can add to our understanding of the words we hear.

---

8. Bradt, *Story as a Way of Knowing*, 6.
9. Quoted in ibid.

Because the context includes much more than just the words, the *words* do not have to convey all the *meaning* by themselves. A storyteller can tip his head, pause, soften his voice, or wince, and the body language will significantly shape the meaning of his words. Ong calls this *infrastructure*: "Oral utterances are given their greater precision by nonverbal elements, which form the infrastructure of the oral utterance."[10] Even written stories usually come with some of this infrastructure, and when they do, the stories are more powerful because they are more comprehensive communication.

Stories Are Safe

Stories are often a safe way to communicate, because the truth embedded in a story can be presented indirectly. Truth is often accepted most easily when it is presented indirectly, as Haddon Robinson illustrates in his classic book on preaching:

> Narratives are most effective when the audience hears the story and arrives at the speaker's ideas without the ideas being stated directly.
>
> Motion picture director Stanley Kubrick discussed the power of the indirect idea in an interview reported in *Time*: "The essence of dramatic form is to let an idea come over people without its being plainly stated. When you say something directly, it is simply not as potent as it is when you allow people to discover it for themselves."[11]

A story that makes its point indirectly sneaks up on our awareness. The initial puzzlement attracts our attention and activates our imagination as we search for meaning.

The indirect approach is potent in a variety of contexts. Elementary school teachers, such as Jerry Ameis, have used it to

---

10. Quoted in ibid., 23.
11. Haddon W. Robinson, *Biblical Preaching,* 2d ed. (Grand Rapids: Baker, 2001), 130–31.

help students solve math problems. Ameis uses books such as *How Many Snails?* to introduce math problems embedded in an adventure story. As the children immerse themselves in the action, the problems faced by the characters become authentic for the children as well.[12] Approaching the subject indirectly diminishes the children's math anxiety and allows them to effectively solve the problems.

Missions professor Tom Steffen encourages missionaries to use an indirect approach when teaching doctrine to tribal people. He believes that missionaries must "become effective storytellers capable of clothing abstract concepts in concrete characters and objects."[13] Clarence Thomson offers a good example of how this "clothing" technique might work in his retelling an old Irish story about God's healing.

> Once upon a time, a long time ago, there was a king in Ireland. Ireland had lots of small kingdoms in those days, and this king's kingdom was one among many. Both king and kingdom were quite ordinary and nobody paid much attention to either of them.
>
> But one day, the king received a huge beautiful diamond from a relative who had died. It was the largest diamond anyone had ever seen. It dazzled everyone. The other kings began to pay attention to him for if he had a diamond like this he must be special. The people, too, came from far and wide to see the diamond. The king had it on constant display in a glass box so that all who wished could come to see and admire it. Of course, armed guards kept a constant vigil. Both king and kingdom prospered, and the king attributed all his good fortune to the diamond.

---

12. Jerry A. Ameis, "Stories Invite Children to Solve Mathematical Problems," *Teaching Children Mathematics* 8, no. 5 (January 2002): 264.
13. Tom A. Steffen, "Rethinking the Role of Narrative in Mission Training," *Occasional Bulletin of the Evangelical Missiological Society* 9, no. 3 (1997): 5.

One day a nervous guard asked to see him. The guard was visibly shaken. He told the king terrible news: the diamond had developed a flaw! A crack right down the middle! The king was horrified and ran to the glass box to see for himself. It was true. The diamond was now flawed terribly.

He called all the jewelers in the land to ask their advice. They gave him only bad news. The flaw was so deep, they said, that if they were to try to sand it down, they would grind it to practically nothing, and if they tried to split it into two still substantial stones, it easily might shatter into a million fragments.

As the king was pondering these terrible options, an old jeweler who had arrived late came to him and said, "If you will give me a week with that stone, I think I can make it better." The king didn't believe him at first because the other jewelers were so sure it couldn't be fixed, but the old man was insistent. Finally the king relented, but said he couldn't let the diamond out of his castle. The old man said that would be all right: he could work there and the guards could stand outside the room where he was working.

The king, having no better solution, agreed to let the old man work. For a week he and the guards hovered about, hearing scratching and gentle pounding and grinding. They wondered what he was doing and what would happen if the old man was tricking them.

Finally, the week was up and the old man came out of the room. King and guards rushed in to see the man's work, and the king burst into tears of joy. It was better! The old man had carved a perfect rose on top of the diamond; and the crack that ran down inside now was the stem of the rose.[14]

---

14. From Clarence Thomson, *Parables and the Enneagram*, 1–2, used with permission of the publisher, Metamorphous Press, PO Box 10606, Portland, OR 97296 (503-228-4972).

We could directly affirm that God takes our deepest flaws and turns them into something beautiful, and some people might be encouraged by that assertion, but it would not have the power of this story, which makes the same point indirectly. Stories activate the imagination by approaching situations indirectly.

Stories Are Interesting

One of the things we like best about stories is that they are so interesting. Part of what makes a story interesting is that there is always a bit of mystery. The sort of story in which we are most interested, the ministry story, should have a clear point, but if it is a good story, the point will be made in a way that invites the hearer to listen to the story more than once. With each repetition, the main point will be reinforced and the hearer may see more details, or think of another way to apply the truth, which will allow him or her to enjoy the story even more. Bello Misal, a Nigerian, recounts a Hausa *misali* (parable) that offers a good example of a story with a bit of mystery:

> There was a hunter who went hunting gorillas. On his way he met a rabbit and shot it. He roasted the rabbit and ate it. After he ate the rabbit he proceeded on his trip until he found a deer. He again shot it, boiled its meat and ate. He kept on doing this to animals until he came to the actual gorillas, but because he had gotten fat, he could not confront the gorillas. Instead the gorillas attacked him and killed him.[15]

Bello reports that the storyteller did not attempt to interpret the parable but continued with other parables. When he was done, the farmers, hunters, rulers, and traders in the audience left

---

15. Bello Melton Misal, "An Interpretation of the Agricultural Parables of the Kingdom in Matthew 13:1–31 in an African Cultural Background" (Th.M. thesis, Biola University, 1990), 24.

for their homes. As they traveled, each group tried to interpret the parable, and each group found a different application.

> The farmers' interpretative point was that if one wants to be a successful farmer he should not plant too many crops in one farm. The hunters' interpretation was that if you want to be a successful hunter do not eat too much or you will be too fat and cannot face wild animals. The rulers and kings who were present thought of the parable as an indication that a successful ruler must be kind to the weaker persons in his domain or else he cannot rule the stronger people in his kingdom.[16]

The essential point of the story is clear—keep the main thing the main thing—but the interesting story activated the hearers' imaginations and provoked a variety of applications.

Looking Back

Story is how we shape our experience into meaning. We live our lives in narrative and make sense of it with stories. Naturally, we use stories in all sorts of ways and in all sorts of situations, especially to explain the unusual. Stories are powerful. We respond to stories instinctively because they come to us as our first knowledge did, wrapped in all the context of verbal communication resonating with how we organize life. Stories are powerful because they are inherently ambiguous, indirect, and connective.

Orleanna, the wife and mother in Barbara Kingsolver's novel *The Poisonwood Bible,* summarized the importance of story this way: "Listen. To live is to be marked. To live is to change, to acquire the words of a story, and that is the only celebration we mortals really know. In perfect stillness, frankly, I've only found sorrow."[17]

---

16. Ibid.
17. Barbara Kingsolver, *The Poisonwood Bible* (New York: HarperCollins, 1998), 385.

CHAPTER TWO

Why We Use Stories

We dream, not in bullet points, but in narratives.
—GORDON G. SHAW

STORIES ARE A UNIVERSAL FORM of communication. No matter where we go, no matter what we are talking about, sooner or later a story is going to become part of the conversation. Often the story will be the most memorable and powerful part of the conversation. We all use stories, but we often do not think about why. In this chapter, I want to explain the theory of story usage, why we tell stories, and offer some examples of how leaders in particular use stories.

Six Basic Reasons to Use Stories

My research shows that we tend to use stories for six basic reasons: (1) to explain the unusual, (2) to teach important things, (3) to make things easier to remember, (4) to help solve problems, (5) to help create identity and community, and (6) to allow us to share the experiences of others.

Stories Explain the Unusual

Perhaps the most basic reason we use stories is to explain the unusual. From birth, we are particularly aware of things that are out of the ordinary. Jerome Bruner explains that infants instinctively notice the unusual, and their desire to explain it is probably what pushes them toward speech.

> Infants reliably perk up in the presence of the unusual: they look more fixedly, stop sucking, show cardiac deceleration, and so on. It is not surprising, then, that when they begin acquiring language they are much more likely to devote their linguistic efforts to what is unusual in their world. They not only perk up in the presence of, but also gesture toward, vocalize, and finally talk about what is unusual.[1]

From the beginning of life, we notice the unusual things around us, and we never grow out of it. In every culture, there is an expected normal behavior. When people behave in a normal way, we do not ask *why*; the behavior is simply taken for granted. However, departures from the ordinary create what Paul Grice calls, "surplus meaning," and that triggers a search for an explanation, which usually produces a story.[2] The story produced probably will attempt to explain the unusual and explain why the unusual event "makes sense." Bruner gives an example:

> If somebody comes into the post office, unfurls the Stars and Stripes, and commences to wave it, [the storyteller] will tell you, in response to your puzzled question, that today is probably some national holiday that he himself had forgotten, that the local American Legion post may be having a fundraiser, or even simply that the man with

---

1. Jerome Bruner, *Acts of Meaning* (Cambridge, MA: Harvard, 1990), 78.
2. Ibid., 48.

the flag is some kind of nationalistic nut whose imagination has been touched by something in this morning's
tabloid.[3]

The story will make sense to us if it explains the unusual. Throughout our lives we tell stories to explain things.

Stories Explain Important Things

Stories also are used to explain important things in memorable
ways. This may be why we tell stories to our children; we want
them to remember what is important. We want them to be faith-
ful like Horton the Elephant, brave like Dorothy in the Wizard
of Oz, and honest like Pinocchio. Stories present information in
"easily digestible form."[4] In fact, the Hasidim consider stories the
best way to teach their children the beliefs and practices of the
community.

Stories are equally useful in helping adults remember the important things. David Silver tells how public health workers in
Uganda used stories to help people understand illness and avoid
disease.[5] In villages without doctors and hospitals, one of the most
common ways for a woman to die is in childbirth. Health workers
wanted to help the traditional birth attendants (midwives) identify the mothers who were most at risk in time to send them to
the hospital, where higher levels of care were available. At first, the
health workers tried to teach the midwives, usually older native
women, using lists of symptoms and words like *anemia, cephalo-
disproportion,* and *malaria* without much success. Someone got
the idea to rework the material into a lively story song, loosely
translated as follows:

---

3. Ibid., 49–50.
4. J. Askham, "Telling Stories," *Sociological Review* 30, no. 4 (1982): 570.
5. David Silver, "Songs and Storytelling: Bringing Health Messages to Life in
   Uganda," *Education for Health: Change in Learning and Practice* 14, no. 1 (2001):
   51–61.

If their eyes are pale, and they're feeling very weak,
   to the hospital, to the hospital;
If their hips are small, and they're looking pretty thin,
   to the hospital, to the hospital;
If their fever's high, and they're having lots of chills,
   to the hospital, to the hospital . . .

With this simple story song, the midwives learned the information and understood it in a way that made it easy to transmit to the rest of the village. Stories teach the important things in simple but powerful ways.

Stories Make Things Easier to Remember

Stories are the way we store our life experiences. Life experiences, and the meaning we attach to those experiences, are not stored in lists of facts or tables of data; they are stored in the form of stories. Our brains organize our experiences and understand what they mean in the form of stories. The stories bring order to our lives. That is why they are so easy to remember. Whenever we hear a story, our minds recognize the opportunity to add order to our lives, to understand something more deeply, so we are instinctively attracted by the story.

Not only are stories the way we organize our own experiences, but they are also the way we usually communicate those experiences to others. When someone asks why we do what we do, we usually provide an explanation in the form of a story. If you asked me, "Why do you iron your own shirts?" I would tell you a story about living with Mrs. McAlmon and doing my own laundry for the first time. I asked her what to do about my wrinkly shirts, and she showed me how to iron them. I might go on to tell how, when my wife went to work and needed help with the household chores, ironing was one of the ways I could help. It was a practical way to show her my appreciation and love. Stories allow us to communicate an experience as well as what we think the experience means. Stories add color and vividness to a particular perspective.

The vitality and descriptiveness make stories easy to repeat and remember. The ability to communicate clearly and memorably makes stories powerful.

Stories Help Solve Problems

When someone has a problem and shares the story of that problem with us, we become part of the search for meaning. Any textbook can give us general truth, but when we face a particular person with a particular problem, we often need a story to connect general truth to a specific solution. Suppose someone begins to tell a story about the funny noise his car is making. We all listen with the memories of the noises our cars have made. His story activates our imaginations by linking our past experiences with his situation. Often that linkage will bring to light a story that may explain the noise.

Physicians do the same sort of thing in the process of diagnosis. During medical school and residency, a physician hears thousands of illness stories that illustrate what a disease looks and sounds like, what might happen as a result of different treatments, and what might go wrong. The stories provide a highly flexible framework for illustrating the lessons of experience and make those lessons easy to remember. A good physician uses the stories he has heard to properly understand the story he is hearing from the patient in front of him. The stories help him understand the problem.

Scientists also use stories to help them understand problems. As they assemble data and try to give it meaning, they inevitably tell stories. Too often they are stories of natural selection and impersonal forces, but the impulse to explain how it all makes sense pushes them into storymaking. Indeed, sometimes a story is the only way to make something understandable to a layperson. I have trouble understanding quantum physics (don't you?), so I was fascinated to read an article by physicist Hans Christian Von Baeyer in which he told several stories with protagonists in quantum situations.[6] There

---

6. Hans Christian Von Baeyer, "Tangled Tales," *Sciences* 41, no. 2 (2001): 14–18.

were the stories of Schrodinger's poor cat, two villainous physicists in Hardy's reprieve, and Vaidman's bead game. These stories helped me understand the extraordinary rules that govern entangled quantum systems. The stories were so odd that I wondered if they were accurate, so I asked a physicist friend of mine to evaluate these stories. Here is part of what he said:

> The stories are good but they are only half the story. The other half is the math. To get the full picture you really need both. . . . After all, the stories and metaphors are both (a) incomplete representations of the underlying reality, and (b) overlaid with the potential for inappropriate extensions that do not map to the underlying reality.[7]

I had to smile. My friend was probably right; the math might help, but without the stories most of us would understand nothing at all. Stories help us understand problems.

Stories Create Identity and Community

We form our experience into meaning with stories, and as those stories accumulate, we begin to understand ourselves. We begin to develop a personal identity, a personal story. The same sort of thing happens in a culture. One way to think about culture is to think of it as a group of people who share similar stories. Americans share similar stories of immigrating to this country, working hard, and becoming successful. We share stories of our war for independence and the westward expansion. The stories we share help us understand things in similar ways. Our daily interactions strengthen and reinforce these commonalities.

When you think about it, most of our social interactions are opportunities to tell and retell stories. When a coworker asks, "What's new?" or a parent asks, "What did you learn in Sunday school?" or a spouse asks, "How was your day?" or a doctor asks,

---

7. Personal conversation with Wesley Downum, Ph.D. physicist, February 5, 2005.

"How have you been?" those questions are invitations to tell a story. Sometimes we tell our own story, and sometimes we tell stories about someone else's story, but it is almost always a story that binds us together and makes us one.

Stories are intrinsically relational, because every story involves at least two people, a teller and a listener. Kevin Bradt calls this "the interdependent transaction of storying."[8] We are familiar with the role of a storyteller, but the listener has an important role as well. A good listener does not simply sit and passively absorb the story; he or she provides a different perspective. As we tell a story, this different perspective is always part of our awareness and consciously or unconsciously influences how we shape the story. If I told you a story about something that happened at church, it would come out differently than if I told the same story to my wife. The story I told you would need lots more detail and explanation than the story I told my wife, because she knows the church situation and you do not. However, both stories would be fundamentally relational.

As we tell our stories to each other, my meaning becomes part of your meaning, and your meaning becomes part of mine. Our shared understanding brings our individual worlds into closer alignment. This potential alignment prompted Thomas Boomershine, a seminary professor and founder of the Network of Biblical Storytellers, to affirm the connective value of storytelling:

> Storytelling creates community. Persons who tell each other stories become friends. And men and women who know the same stories deeply are bound together in special ways. . . . Good stories get retold and form an ever expanding storytelling network. . . . New connections are established between persons who have heard and identi-

---

8. Kevin M. Bradt, *Story as a Way of Knowing* (Kansas City, MO: Sheed & Ward, 1997), 11.

fied with the same stories. . . . The deeper the meaning of
the story, the deeper are the relationships that are formed
by the sharing.[9]

Stories are intrinsically relational. One aspect of their power is
the ability to deepen relationships and create community.

Stories Allow Us to Share the Experiences of Others

When we hear a story, the experience described in the story
becomes part of our experience, and the meaning becomes part
of our wisdom. Through a story, we can imaginatively enter into
a very different world, shift to a different viewpoint, and begin
to experience what someone else has experienced. One of the
amazing things about stories is that they can be real or imaginary
without any loss of power. We will never be little pigs, but we can
share their experiences—the fear of a hungry enemy outside and
the security of a sturdy house. Susan Shaw, in her comprehensive
book about storytelling, points out that *Star Wars* resonates with
earthbound humans because it deals with common experiences,
such as losing one's family, searching for one's identity, and strug-
gling to do good. Shaw goes on to explain:

> Identification with a story allows the learners to
> experience the specifics of a story vicariously. This
> experience creates space for the learners to learn from
> the story's experience as if they had actually participated
> in it—which they have, imaginatively, through the story.
> Stories, therefore, are an experiential learning process,
> involving cognitive, affective, and behavioral modes of
> learning, so that learners participate in stories, reflect
> on them, understand them, create meaning of them,
> and act on them. In so doing, learners reorder their own

---

9. Thomas E. Boomershine, *Story Journey: An Invitation to the Gospel as Storytelling*
   (Nashville: Abingdon, 1988), 18–19.

experiences—cognitive, affective, and behavioral—into meaningful patterns and responses.[10]

Stories help us to experience vicariously what others have experienced and share the meaning of those experiences.

Stories mediate a specific sort of knowledge—experiential knowledge. Stories are powerful because they allow us to participate in situations that are totally apart from our own experience. In *Tom Sawyer*, we can identify with a young man growing up on the banks of the Mississippi River. In *Star Trek*, we can identify with a spaceship crew going where no man has gone before. In *Harry Potter*, we can identify with a young orphan learning to be a good magician. In *Chicken Little*, we can identify with a paranoid chicken. In *Charlotte's Web*, we can identify with a pregnant spider. This experience is obviously vicarious, but even vicarious experience is experience. Experience creates meaning, and meaning provides the potential for personal transformation.

The same sort of thing happens with biblical stories. Through the prophet Nathan's story, we can enter into the palace intrigue of ancient Israel. Through the stories of Jesus, we can enter into first-century Palestine and identify with widows, farmers, and Samaritans. Lynne Tirrell believes that this ability to experience "sentiments not our own" is one of the most significant ways that stories help us to develop morally. "Through telling and listening to stories, we learn to make subtle and not so subtle shifts in point of view, and these shifts are crucial to developing the sense of self and other so necessary to moral agency."[11] Stories allow us to make these shifts in point of view and to vicariously experience situations that are totally outside of our reality.

---

10. Susan M. Shaw, *Storytelling in Religious Education* (Birmingham, AL: Religious Education Press, 1999), 54.

11. Lynne Tirrell, "Storytelling and Moral Agency," *Journal of Aesthetics and Art Criticism* 48, no. 2 (1990): 119.

Why Leaders Use Stories

Everyone uses stories, but leaders have particular impact when they use stories. There is a growing body of evidence that shows that the most effective leaders are those who tell lots of stories.

Jesus Used Stories

Part of what made Jesus such an effective teacher and leader were the stories he told. Jesus lived in a largely oral society (some estimates suggest that only five percent of his hearers were literate), so stories were a familiar way to learn and impart knowledge. When Jesus wanted to make a point, he didn't give a lecture; he told a story.[12] Jesus told stories for the same reasons we have seen already—because they are a powerful way to convey a message, they are easy to remember, they create unity around what is important, and they inspire. The characters and situations in the stories were familiar to his audiences: only the insights were unusual. Jesus used these ministry stories so extensively that Mark observed, "He did not say anything to them without using a parable" (Mark 4:34).

The Church Uses Stories

Given that the Lord of the church loved stories, it does not surprise us to recognize that stories had a profound role in forming the church. In the beginning, there were no written texts—no Gospels, no Epistles. Instead, the apostles and other eyewitnesses told what they had seen. They shared their experiences and formed meaning. In other words, they told stories, true stories, which were collected and written down under the inspiration of the Holy Spirit. Luke explains the process in the introduction to his gospel:

---

12. Robert Jacks, late professor of homiletics at Princeton Seminary, noticed that and marveled, "How odd that we tend to take Jesus' stories and turn them into lectures." G. Robert Jacks, *Just Say the Word: Writing for the Ear* (Grand Rapids: Eerdmans, 1996), 7.

Many have undertaken to draw up an account of the things that have been fulfilled among us, just as they were handed down to us by those who from the first were eyewitnesses and servants of the word. Therefore, since I myself have carefully investigated everything from the beginning, it seemed good also to me to write an orderly account for you, most excellent Theophilus, so that you may know the certainty of the things you have been taught. (Luke 1:1–4)

In the progressive revelation of Scripture, the story of Jesus became the latest, best part of God's story, the Bible.

Story is a particularly effective way of conveying profound insight, which has led some to insist that the gospel had to be conveyed in the form of a story. Frederick Borsch, professor of New Testament at Lutheran Theological Seminary in Philadelphia, suggests, "Story offers a way of talking about what otherwise cannot fully be brought to expression."[13] Borsch explains that the stories in the Bible are the best way, and sometimes the only way, to reflect on the meaning of the mystery of God's presence. Susan Shaw develops this same idea by suggesting that even theology "is a reflection upon religious experiences that are first expressed in narrative form."[14] She points out that theology may systematize and organize the material in the stories, but the system and the organization can never be completely detached from the underlying narrative. She concludes, "Theological ideas are always tied to religious stories."[15]

Don Dent, writing from a missionary's perspective, believes that evangelism is most appealing and effective when it is done with stories.

---

13. Frederick Houk Borsch, *Many Things in Parables: Extravagant Stories of New Community* (Philadelphia: Fortress, 1988), 4.
14. Shaw, *Storytelling in Religious Education*, 78.
15. Ibid.

Stories are loved in all societies. However, our literate, Western, evangelical heritage has often summarized the message of salvation into short statements of proposi- tional truth. Though true, they have little appeal to many of the world's people. Even in the U.S., many people are more open [to] and more deeply impacted by stories. This is even truer of oral learners and functionally illiterate people who make up a large percentage of the world's population. Telling a series of Bible stories involves people over time and leads them step-by-step to the Savior.[16]

Stories make evangelism more attractive and effective. They form the foundation of our theology and are the building blocks of God's revelation.

Business Leaders Use Stories

A growing body of evidence suggests that business leaders also are more effective if they tell stories. Sheldon Buckler and Karen Zien conducted extensive research on mature, innovative companies and were surprised at how extensively stories were used by the most effective leaders. Buckler and Zien reported that they found four types of leaders in these companies. The first type had no stories, only business plans and numerical goals. These leaders were clear enough, but their style had no "soul." The second type told old stories about "the good old days." These leaders made the history come alive, but their stories made most people feel left out because they had not been present to be part of those stories. The third type of leader, "the innovative leader," shaped the old stories to fit the existing situation and showed how the past could inspire the future. This was a very effective way to use stories. The fourth type of leader, "the transformational leader," invented, embodied, and continually reformed new stories about new futures. This was the most powerful way that leaders used

---

16. Don Dent, "Making It Stick," *Evangelical Missions Quarterly* 40, no. 2 (2004): 153.

stories.[17] Transformational leaders used stories to explain what was important and to create unity and common purpose. The results of their research led Buckler and Zien to offer this clear advice to leaders: "Tell these stories everywhere . . . in staff meetings, individual interviews and conversations, corporate events, and outside speaking engagements."[18]

Effective Church Leaders Use Stories

Prominent church leaders echo Buckler and Zien's advice. Leith Anderson advises pastors to "keep a list of blessings and successes. Thank God for them on a regular basis. Tell and retell these stories in the church. It is a necessary spiritual discipline."[19] Henry and Richard Blackaby observe, "Wise leaders continually help their people see how God is working in their midst. Leaders can do this by telling stories—true stories of how God has worked in the past and how God is working at present."[20] The stories help people understand what is important. Erwin McManus enthusiastically affirms the role of story in the life of the church: "The stories you choose to tell inform the emerging culture. Stories that are rooted in the life of the congregation breathe life into the congregation. Great leaders are great storytellers. Great churches have great stories. Great stories create a great future."[21]

To create this "great future," leaders must intentionally accept the role of storyteller. Blackaby and Blackaby remind us, "The leader is a symbol as well as a 'keeper of the stories' concerning what God has been doing in that organization. It is said that revival is spread on the wings of the testimonies of those whose lives

17. Sheldon A. Buckler and Karen Anne Zien, "The Spirituality of Innovation: Learning from Stories," *Journal of Product Innovation Management* 13 (1996): 405.
18. Ibid., 394.
19. Leith Anderson, *Leadership That Works* (Grand Rapids: Bethany, 1999), 171.
20. Henry T. Blackaby and Richard Blackaby, *Spiritual Leadership: Moving People on to God's Agenda* (Nashville: Broadman & Holman, 2001), 79.
21. Erwin Raphael McManus, *An Unstoppable Force: Daring to Become the Church God Had in Mind* (Loveland, CO: Group, 2001), 122.

have been changed in revival. The leader is both the messenger and the message."[22]

Stories emphasize the empowering parts of the past and bring them into the present in a way that creates a common understanding of what the ministry or business is all about. Tom Steffen goes so far as to suggest that the best way to understand a church is to collect the stories they tell. "From the collective *stories* of people the *story* (characterization) of the church will emerge. . . . [This characterization]—usually deliberate in nature—distinguishes a church's traits and disposition."[23]

The recitation of corporate stories is an effective way to incorporate new members. In the church, Blackaby and Blackaby suggest, this is most effectively done by telling four types of stories: stories about the church members, stories about the organization's history, stories about the values of the organization, and stories about the culture of the organization.[24] Erwin McManus gives a testimony about how this works:

> I also began to realize that whenever I affirmed someone through a story, it helped shape the culture. If I told stories of the secret servanthood of members in the body, it inspired everyone else to serve. When I celebrated sacrificial giving by individuals, it inspired others to give sacrificially. The power of blessing that the Bible talks about is something very real and very important. A part of spiritual leadership is rewarding those things that Christ would reward, blessing those who are reflecting Christ, and inspiring everyone to follow that example.[25]

Excellent pastors, like Bill Hybels of Willow Creek Community Church, seem to inspire people almost instinctively. Notice how

---

22. Blackaby and Blackaby, *Spiritual Leadership,* 80.
23. Tom A. Steffen, "Congregational Character: From Stories to Story," *Journal of the American Society for Church Growth* 11, no. 2 (2000): 17.
24. Blackaby and Blackaby, *Spiritual Leadership,* 161.
25. McManus, *Unstoppable Force,* 142.

the following story reflects and reinforces the values of Willow Creek.

I had just finished presenting my weekend message at Willow and I was standing in the bullpen, talking to people. A young married couple approached me, placed a blanketed bundle in my arms, and asked me to pray for their baby.

As I asked what the baby's name was, the mother pulled back the blanket that had covered the infant's face. I felt my knees begin to buckle. I thought I was going to faint. Had the father not steadied me I may well have keeled over. In my arms was the most horribly deformed baby I had ever seen. The whole center of her tiny face was caved in. How she kept breathing I will never know.

All I could say was, "Oh my . . . oh my . . . oh my."

"Her name is Emily," said the mother. "We've been told she has about six weeks to live," added the father. "We would like you to pray that before she dies she will know and feel our love."

Barely able to mouth the words, I whispered, "Let's pray." Together we prayed for Emily. Oh, did we pray. As I handed her back to her parents I asked, "Is there anything we can do for you, any way that we as a church can serve you during this time?"

The father responded with words that still amaze me. He said, "Bill, we're okay. Really we are. We've been in a loving small group for years. Our group members knew that this pregnancy had complications. They were at our house the night we learned the news, and they were at the hospital when Emily was delivered. They helped us absorb the reality of the whole thing. They even cleaned our house and fixed our meals when we brought her home. They pray for us constantly and call us several times every day. They're even helping us plan Emily's funeral."

Just then three other couples stepped forward and surrounded Emily and her parents. "We always attend church together as a group," said one of the group members.

It was a picture I will carry to my grave, a tight-knit huddle of loving brothers and sisters doing their best to soften one of the cruelest blows life can throw. After a group prayer, they all walked up the side aisle toward our lobby.[26]

Stories are used by leaders to emphasize what is important. When they do that well, they create a unified community.

Looking Back

All of us use stories to explain the unusual, clarify the important, remember the necessary, solve problems, create and strengthen community, and share each other's experiences. The most effective leaders use stories. Jesus used stories; the church, modern business leaders, and effective pastors do so as well. When leaders use stories effectively, they inspire and unify their communities.

---

26. Bill Hybels, *Courageous Leadership* (Grand Rapids: Zondervan, 2002), 22–23.

CHAPTER THREE

How to Put a Story Together

I don't believe anyone knows exactly how "he makes things up." Making up is a very mysterious thing.

—C. S. LEWIS

IF YOU ASKED ME HOW TO BUILD a house, I would start my answer with something general. I would tell you to put the foundation at the bottom, the walls in the middle, and the roof on the top. That answer might be enough if you were vaguely curious about houses. But if you were actually going to build a house, and you knew that I used to be an engineer, you might want more details. You might want to know about soil-bearing capacity, foundation loads, wall strength, truss loading, roof slope, and lots more. Builders need more details.

If we want to build stories, we need more details about how it's done. If we want to put together a story, we need to understand more than beginning, middle, and end. We need to know all the parts of a story and how they go together.

In this chapter, we will look at what the experts have to teach us about the elements of story and how they fit together. I will start with some general advice and move on to more detailed advice.

General Advice

The most effective stories are relatively short, fairly simple, very clear, sensual, coherent, and to the point. Let me expand a bit on each of these elements.

Effective Stories Are Short

Nancy Mellon, a renowned storyteller, reminds us that all the great old fairy tales can be told in a short amount of time. "A story, which fills fifteen minutes with well-chosen words and a truly satisfactory composition of characters and events, can give joy for a whole lifetime."[1] Freelance writer Bonnie Durrance puts it even more succinctly: "Keep your story short. Don't get tangled up trying to write a novel."[2]

Effective Stories Are Simple

Effective stories do not have very many characters, and we quickly learn what the characters are doing and why. In "The Three Little Pigs," there are three pigs, not twenty. They build three houses. A wolf is trying to eat them. It is pretty simple. In the parable of the Wise and Foolish Builders, there are two builders, not twelve. One builds on sand. The other builds on rock. There is a storm—and consequences. It is fairly simple.

Effective Stories Are Clear

An effective story is clear in the sense that we quickly grasp what is going on. There is a single perspective from which the story develops. The speech is direct. Characters do things. Tangents and side issues are minimized or eliminated.

---

1. Nancy Mellon, *Storytelling and the Art of Imagination* (Cambridge, MA: Yellow Moon, 1992), 176.
2. Bonnie Durrance, "Stories at Work," *Training and Development* 51, no. 2 (1997): 28.

Effective Stories Are Sensual

An effective story engages our senses. John Walsh, a pastor and storyteller, writes, "The goal of a story is to stimulate the listener's five senses, to draw them into the story. There should be enough description so the audience will see, hear, taste, smell, and feel everything going on."[3]

Effective Stories Are Coherent

In an effective story, we quickly know what to expect. The story plays by the rules. In *Aesop's Fables,* animals talk. In *The Iliad,* they do not. In *Peter Pan,* boys can fly. In *Tom Sawyer,* they cannot. An experienced listener can quickly adjust to the most outlandish story universe if the story is coherent within that universe.

Effective Stories Are Pointed

Finally, effective stories have a point. A really good story *embodies* the point. Susan Shaw puts it like this: "A story . . . does not contain the answer but is the answer."[4] One of the benefits of original stories is that we can create them to provide the precise answers we intend to give. Mark Galli and Craig Brian Larson call this "control."

> The benefit of fictional stories, though, is control: we can tailor them to our specific needs and tastes. Unlike true stories that we have to take as is, we can craft a fictional story as Jesus did his parables, to have the characters say and do precisely what we need them to do and say.[5]

As we learn this sort of control, the answers we provide are better and more powerful.

3. John Walsh, *The Art of Storytelling: Easy Steps to Presenting an Unforgettable Story* (Chicago: Moody, 2003), 71.
4. Susan M. Shaw, *Storytelling in Religious Education* (Birmingham, AL: Religious Education Press, 1999), 56.
5. Mark Galli and Craig Brian Larson, *Preaching That Connects* (Grand Rapids: Zondervan, 1994), 62.

More Details

Dan Allender, a Christian counselor who has listened to many stories, reflects that every good story begins in the same place and has the same general shape. "Every good story begins with innocence. Then there is tragedy, where innocence is lost. Then there is tension, where life is threatened. Finally, there is resolution, when the bad guy is destroyed."[6] Perhaps this shape comes from the story of creation itself. We began in the Garden. Then there was the tragedy of the Fall, and the consequences of sin—death. Then Jesus came and redeemed us. Perhaps the shape of that original story shapes all the subsequent smaller stories. Regardless of where the shape comes from, storymakers use six elements to create this shape—characters, context, plot, climax, resolution, and result. We need to look carefully at each one of these.

Characters

Most experts advise storymakers to start with the characters. They need to be believable or "invite the willing suspension of belief."[7] In The Chronicles of Narnia, C. S. Lewis creates such believable characters—beavers, fauns, witches, and the wonderful lion—that we willingly suspend belief in *reality* (where animals do not act this way or talk) to enter into the story. Characters do things, they look at the world in particular ways, have strengths and weaknesses, and develop as the story unfolds. A character becomes believable, not with explanations and descriptions, but by doing things, going places, wearing things, and saying things. Mark Powell observes, "Readers [or listeners] are most likely to empathize with characters who are similar to them (realistic empathy) or with characters who represent what they would like to be (idealistic empathy)."[8]

---

6. Dan B. Allender, "The Wounded Heart" (speech, Covenant Seminary, St. Louis, 1998).
7. Shaw, *Storytelling in Religious Education*, 292.
8. Mark A. Powell, *What Is Narrative Criticism?* (Minneapolis, MN: Fortress, 1990), 56.

Perhaps the simplest way to develop a character is to give it a symbolic name. After all, every name contains a story (Hitler, Gandhi, Esther, Saddam) that evokes a positive or negative feeling and expectation. Nancy Mellon suggests that even the sound of a name can evoke certain feelings (see table 1).[9]

TABLE 1

Sound	Example	Feeling Evoked
"ah"	Ali Baba, Fatima, Hans	Opening
"o"	[Dumbo]	Inclusiveness
"oo"	[Pooh]	Wonder mixed with fear
"ee"	[Nemo]	Strong sense of identity
Quick little syllables	[Tootsie, Bambi]	Playful, lighthearted
Strong consonants	k, t, j, f	Willful, intense
Soft flowing sounds	b, n, m, l	Gentle

We may wonder whether the sounds evoke the suggested feeling or the feelings are already associated with the name, but the whole idea is evocative and supports the point that names are significant. Characters are the first story element.

Context

The action of the story takes place somewhere, and the shape of that somewhere—the context—will shape the story. Where a story happens will influence what the characters may and may not do there. According to Susan Shaw, "The setting [context] creates certain parameters of action, while at the same time stimulating responses from the characters that inhabit that setting."[10] Context sets limits to what can, or might, happen. If the story is set on a desert island, for example, we will expect the characters to deal with lots of sunshine, extreme heat, and isolation. If the story is set in a jungle, we will expect the characters to be affected by the copious rain, lush foliage, and lurking tigers. Narnia in the winter is significantly different from Narnia in the spring. Nancy

---

9. Mellon, *Storytelling and the Art of Imagination*, 12.
10. Shaw, *Storytelling in Religious Education*, 293.

Mellon makes the obvious point that each season evokes a different feeling that storymakers can take advantage of. Winter evokes a mood of reflection and stillness. Spring sets a mood of joyous rediscovery. Summer tends to be a buoyant time, with long days and warm nights. Autumn tends to bring the mood down again with culmination, harvest, and preparation for another winter.[11] The context frames the story. It sets the limits of what can happen and helps us predict what the characters might do.

Plot

Plot answers the "what happened" question. The plot begins when a character is plunged into a situation. Some have suggested that there are only a few basic plots and that all stories are variations on one of these:

- Adventure: Hero overcomes a challenge and wins reward.
- Romance: Hero overcomes a challenge and wins love.
- Tragedy: Hero fails to overcome challenge and meets downfall.
- Melodrama: Polarized battle between hero and villain.
- Irony: Hero turns out to be a villain.
- Comedy: Hero turns out to be a fool.

Plot establishes certain expectations. In an adventure story, no matter how harrowing the adventure, we expect a happy ending where the hero wins the reward. In a romance, even if the princess is in a remote castle surrounded by a moat and guarded by a dragon, we expect the prince to eventually rescue the princess and live happily ever after. The plot establishes this expectation.

When a story does not go according to expectation, we immediately notice and our interest is aroused even more. In a romance, if the princess bites a poison apple and apparently dies, we begin to wonder how the prince will rescue her. When Aslan is killed in

---

11.   Mellon, *Storytelling and the Art of Imagination*, 76.

Narnia, we wonder how spring will ever come. Technically, this plot device is called *contingency*, the unexpected thing that might happen. Any interesting plot must have some element of contingency—tension, ambiguity, threat, or surprise. A good plot must have an element of the unexpected that makes us wonder what is going to happen next. If it doesn't, we will lose interest and stop paying attention.

Climax

Sooner or later, the situation the characters are in must come to a climax. The tension builds until something snaps. The river rises and finally overflows its banks. The opposing forces finally meet in battle. The cops catch up with the robbers. Sooner or later, the plot must come to a climax where things change.

Resolution

After the climax, there is resolution. If the climax is a battle, someone eventually wins. If a farmer plants seed in different kinds of soil, eventually there is resolution—harvest comes and we see what happens. Every story must resolve sooner or later. Mickey Spillane, the famous mystery writer, noted, "The most important part of a story is the ending. No one reads a book to get to the middle."[12]

Nancy Mellon makes the odd but intriguing suggestion that there is a basic rhythm to this resolution. She suggests that many classic stories unfold in a sort of pulse beat, "a regular flow of fours," and the fourth beat is the resolution.[13] She explains that the central character may set out on a journey, face and overcome one obstacle, then a second obstacle, and a third, but the next event, the fourth "pulse beat," will be one of resolution or victory. We could think of examples, such as "The Three Little Pigs," where the Big Bad Wolf attacks three times and then falls down

---

12. Quoted in "Quotable Quotes," *Reader's Digest,* November 2002.
13. Mellon, *Storytelling and the Art of Imagination,* 178. Although she makes no reference to it, this pattern is also in evidence in Proverbs 30:15, 18, 21, and 29.

the chimney on the fourth beat, thus eliminating the threat to the three little pigs.

We also can see this four-beat pattern in the parables of Jesus. In the parable of the Sower, for example, there were three "bad" soils, but the fourth soil was "good soil" that produced abundantly. In the parable of the Good Samaritan, the man on the journey encounters three "pulse beats" who do not help—the thieves, the priest, and the Levite. The fourth beat—the Samaritan—is the one who helps.

Mellon goes on to suggest that this basic four-beat pattern can be doubled or tripled. In a double four-beat, the hero faces seven obstacles before he attains victory on the eighth (the second fourth beat). Mellon suggests that this pattern resonates with basic creation rhythms, such as the seven tones of a major scale, seven colors of the rainbow, or seven days of the week. When the basic pulse beat is tripled, the hero will not be victorious until the twelfth event. Mellon sees this pattern as resonating with basic rhythms like the signs of the zodiac, the twelve days of Christmas, or the twelve months of the year.[14] These four-beat patterns may be as subtle as your pulse, but in a story they provide an intrinsic rhythm that brings the plot to resolution.

Result

The final element of a story is the result. How do things turn out? The result is the "happily ever after" part of the story. Like the Cheshire Cat's smile in the Alice in Wonderland stories, the result is what's left when the rest is gone. Sometimes, the result is stated overtly, like the moral of the story in *Aesop's Fables*. Typically, however, a story is more powerful when the result is simply implied: "He who has ears, let him hear" (Matt. 11:15). The most powerful stories are often ones in which the point is not stated at all. These stories are seeds, planted in our minds, which may grow into insight sometime, somewhere, somehow.

---

14.   Ibid.

Looking Back

Powerful stories are relatively short, fairly simple, very clear, sensual, and coherent. They also have an obvious point. They are composed of six basic elements: characters, context, plot, climax, resolution, and result. Any visit to any library makes it clear that these six elements can be put together in a nearly infinite variety of ways. We want to see how to put these elements together to make a particular type of story—a ministry story. It is to that task that we now turn.

CHAPTER FOUR

Special Ministry Stories

Jesus was not a theologian. He was God who told stories.
—MADELEINE L'ENGLE'S FRIEND

FOR OUR PURPOSES HERE, WE ARE most interested in ministry stories, the special type of story that is particularly effective in ministry. The most obvious examples of ministry stories are the parables that Jesus told. The very word *parable* is inextricably associated with Jesus, who presented at least one-third of his teaching in the form of parables. Because parables were an integral part of Christ's ministry, if we understand parables in particular, we will be better able to understand ministry stories in general.

In this chapter, we will take a close look at parables. We will start by looking at what the biblical authors meant when they used the term *parable*, where parables came from, and their common characteristics. Next, we will look at some other types of ministry stories—cousins to the parables, if you will—especially the cousin called *fable*. From all of that, we will be ready to make some suggestions about why Jesus used parables so often.

The Ministry Stories Called Parables

Probably more has been written about parables than any other biblical genre, but no clear consensus has emerged on how to define a parable. Part of the problem is that the terms for *parable* in Hebrew and Greek are broad ones. The Hebrew word, *mashal* (plural *meshalim*),[1] and its Septuagint Greek translation, *parabolé*,[2] refer to a wide variety of figurative language. *Meshalim* may be sayings, mocking bywords, similitudes, riddles, allegories, oracles, fables, or proverbs.[3] However, even with this breadth of meaning, *mashal* is never used in reference to a short ministry story, what we would call in English a *parable*. Instead, most of the time in the Old Testament, *mashal* is translated with the English word *proverb* (forty out of fifty-eight occurrences in the New International Version).[4] Proverbs are designed to help a person acquire wisdom, understanding, and insight, and they do that by provoking thought.

The translators of the Greek Old Testament (the Septuagint) rendered the Hebrew term *mashal* as *parabolé,* and thus the meaning of *parabolé* in the Septuagint parallels the broad meaning of *mashal.* Moreover, the meaning of the Greek term itself is also very broad. *Parabolé* is used for proverbs, maxims, metaphorical sayings, enigmatic sayings, rules, parables, symbols, and riddles.[5] Obviously, many of these meanings overlap, which may have been what provoked Craig Evans, a distinguished professor at Trinity Western University, to offer this elegant summary of the etymology of *parabolé*: "One thing [all the meanings] have in common is that they are the opposite of plain speech."[6]

1. *Mashal* is a transliteration of the Hebrew מָשָׁל (plural is מְשָׁלִים).
2. *Parabolé* is a transliteration of the Greek παραβολή.
3. Arland J. Hultgren, *The Parables of Jesus: A Commentary* (Grand Rapids: Eerdmans, 2000), 5.
4. Indeed, the title of the book of Proverbs is actually מִשְׁלֵי שְׁלֹמֹה, which could be rendered, "the *Mishalim* of Solomon."
5. Joachim Jeremias, *The Parables of Jesus,* 2d rev. ed. (Upper Saddle River, NJ: Prentice Hall, 1972), 20.
6. Craig A. Evans, "Parables in Early Judaism," in *The Challenge of Jesus' Parables,* ed. Richard N. Longenecker (Grand Rapids: Eerdmans, 2000), 54.

The Origin of Parables

There is a spirited scholarly discussion about the origin of parables. It is true that there is no extant evidence of any teacher prior to Jesus using the short ministry story we call a parable. It is also true that this form of teaching flourished in the generations that followed Jesus. These truths have led some scholars to claim quite firmly that Jesus invented this sort of teaching. I think we should be a bit more cautious. Apparently, Jesus was the first to use this form of communication in an extensive way, but it is just as apparent that his disciples were familiar with this sort of teaching. The disciples did not ask Jesus *what* he was doing teaching the people in parables; they asked him *why* he was doing it (Matt. 13:10). Kenneth Bailey, a research scholar specializing in the cultural background and literary forms of the New Testament, points out that Jesus lived in a culture that created meaning with simile, metaphor, proverb, and parable.[7] Because meaning in that culture was created metaphorically, we are safe in assuming that others in that culture were creating parables in or shortly before the time of Christ.

Of course, Jesus could have created his parables spontaneously under the inspiration of the Holy Spirit, but it is much more likely that he created these stories much as we would, by adapting and improving a teaching technique that was already in use. In so doing, he would have been consistent with his commitment to humbly submit to the constraints of his incarnation and only use powers available to humankind in general. It seems likely that Jesus obtained his inspiration from at least three sources: fictitious tales and fables that were circulating in first-century culture; actual events that could be adapted to illustrate a theme; or proverbs or wisdom verses that could be developed into stories.[8]

---

7. Kenneth E. Bailey, *Finding the Lost: Cultural Keys to Luke 15* (St. Louis: Concordia, 1992), 16.
8. Brad H. Young, *Jesus and His Jewish Parables: Rediscovering the Roots of Jesus' Teaching* (Mahwah, NJ: Paulist, 1989), 237.

Even if the origins are debated, there is no denying that Jesus was the master of this form of communication. All his parables were original, and he used them to answer questions, justify his teaching, defend his actions, or challenge the words and actions of his opponents.[9]

The Four Characteristics of Parables

Scholars have struggled to provide a simple, comprehensive definition of parable. I think that theologian C. H. Dodd offers the most helpful one:

> At its simplest the parable is a metaphor or simile drawn from nature or common life, arresting the hearer by its vividness or strangeness, and leaving the mind in sufficient doubt about its precise application to tease it into active thought.[10]

This definition reveals four important things that characterize parables—two elements and two effects:

- comparison ("metaphor or simile"),
- source ("drawn from nature or common life"),
- arresting ("arresting the hearer by its vividness or strangeness"),
- stimulating ("leaving the mind in sufficient doubt about its precise application to tease it into active thought").

We need a better understanding of each of these.

Comparison

At the heart of every parable is a comparison—something is being compared to something else, whether by metaphor or

---

9. David B. Gowler, *What Are They Saying About the Parables?* (Mahwah, NJ: Paulist, 2000), 9; Young, *Jesus and His Jewish Parables*, 55.
10. Quoted in Gowler, *What Are They Saying About the Parables?* 7.

simile.[11] The kingdom of heaven is compared to a mustard seed or yeast or a treasure. Parables are created and told to make these comparisons.

Source

Parables are sourced in nature or common life, which makes them slightly different from other types of symbolic stories (such as myths, fables, or fairy tales). Parables could really happen. Parables are rooted in reality. The challenge we face with Jesus' parables is that the "common life" of first-century Palestine is not the common life of today. When Jesus told his stories, the audience shared his social context and had access to enormous insight that we lack on this end of history. Bailey explains it this way:

> Any story that is told to a particular audience at a particular time speaks uniquely to that original audience. . . . This is why interpretation is necessary. For Jesus' original audience the parable was like a political cartoon—the full weight of its message was clear to any perceptive listener who shared the language, religion, history, and culture of the speaker.[12]

Fortunately, a careful study of history and culture can produce an accurate understanding of what life was like for those first hearers, and that understanding leads to accurate interpretation and full participation.

Arresting

Parables may be sourced in the common life, but the situations they present are so vivid or so strange that they arrest our attention. We stop to look. A Samaritan stops to help a Jewish stranger. A son demands his inheritance before his father's death. A treasure

---

11. A *metaphor* equates two things in order to invite comparison: "Joe is a snake." A *simile* is a comparison that uses the word *like* or *as*: "Joe is like a snake."
12. Bailey, *Finding the Lost*, 49.

is discovered in a field. These situations are so strange that we have to stop and look. A parable has this arresting quality.

Stimulating

Parables are not transparently simple, but they are not totally opaque either. A parable is stimulating. It almost compels the audience to apply its message. In fact, when a parable refuses to state its message directly, it actually becomes more effective in persuading the audience of its essential truth. As the parable deliberately gives the impression of insufficiency, the audience becomes actively involved in deducing the meaning and figuring out the application. The parable creates a dialogue between teller and hearer, and the dialogue opens the door to influence and potential change. Parables make us think. They make us see another point of view, and often they convince us to change.

Other Types of Ministry Stories

Although parables are the most familiar type of ministry story, they are not the only type. If parables are a family, they have lots of cousins. Meeting these cousins will give us a better idea of the range of ministry stories that are available.

Family Resemblances

We are often able to distinguish a parable from one of its cousins, but we can rarely do that on form alone. One common characteristic of all these types of stories is that they make some sort of comparison. Harvey McArthur and Robert Johnston provide the following list in their book about rabbinic parables:

- Bywords: Comparisons that describe a person. "He has the patience of Job" or "She has the faith of Abraham."
- Proverbs: Very short comparisons, usually containing an aphorism or very succinct nugget of wisdom.
- Parabolic actions: Object lessons. The action is compared with some lesson or revelation: Jeremiah wearing a yoke

(Jer. 27) or Agabus tying his hands with Paul's belt (Acts 21).

- Similes: Very similar to parables, usually distinguished by length. Parables are longer than similes.
- Metaphors: McArthur and Johnston suggest that metaphors can be distinguished from similes and parables by form. I cannot agree. I think parables are extended metaphors.
- Anecdotes: Stories that are reputed to be about historical figures (for example, the story of George Washington cutting down the cherry tree).
- Example stories: Similar to anecdotes but without any names. The story of the Good Samaritan is often classified as an example story.
- Analogies: A form of comparison wherein one similarity infers other similarities. The comparison of King David to a shepherd infers that he leads, protects, provides, etc.
- Vertical comparisons: Often the ways of God are compared with the ways of kings or other leaders.
- Fables: Very similar to parables, but with animal characters acting like people.[13]

All of these story forms share a family resemblance to parables, but one of these cousins, the fable, is so similar that it deserves special attention.

Fables

Like parables, fables are short stories intended to teach a lesson or provide an insight. A fable uses animal characters metaphorically, attributing human emotions, reasoning, and behavior to the animals in the story. Fables are one of the most ancient forms of story. The Sumerians (second millennium B.C.E.) used fables. Fables appear in early Greek literature and were also popular in

---

13.   Harvey K. McArthur and Robert M. Johnston, *They Also Taught in Parables* (Grand Rapids: Zondervan, 1990), 99–101.

ancient India. They were popularized in anthologies, the most familiar of which is usually attributed to Aesop.

Although fables and parables are similar, they have some strategic differences. Fables are stories about animals behaving like people, whereas parables are about people in more or less realistic settings. Jesus did not tell any stories that we would classify as fables, but the rabbinic literature is full of fables (especially about foxes).[14]

In Western culture, fables often provide a way to communicate a particularly sensitive lesson. Somehow, a story about animals provides a bit more emotional distance than a story about people, and that distance may allow the hearer to more easily accept the point being made. That may be why expert storytellers, such as C. S. Lewis, tell some of their most powerful stories (e.g., The Chronicles of Narnia) using animal protagonists.

Looking Back

Parables are short ministry stories that use metaphor to teach a lesson or provide an insight in a vivid, intriguing way. They were popularized in the first century, when Jesus used them extensively to fulfill his mission of seeking and saving the lost. The Bible contains examples of other types of ministry stories, such as fables. After the time of Jesus, fables (often called parables) became especially popular with the rabbis. These ministry stories were and are very powerful communication tools. In the next chapter we will look at what "makes them work."

---

14. It should be noted that the rabbis did not differentiate between fables and parables and referred to both types of stories as parables.

CHAPTER FIVE

How a Ministry Story Works

God made man because He loves stories.
—ELIE WIESEL

DIFFERENT TYPES OF STORIES HAVE different shapes. Fairy tales often begin with "Once upon a time . . ." and end with "they all lived happily ever after." The ministry stories that we call parables often share a common shape that we can discern in the stories that Jesus told and that shape becomes even more obvious in the rabbinic parables that developed in the centuries that followed. In this chapter, we will explore that shape and notice the elements that constitute parables. Understanding how Jesus and the rabbis put parables together will help us understand why these ministry stories were so effective.

How a Parable Works

Parables are stories that use figurative language to convey truth. John Dominic Crossan, in his helpful discussion of figurative language, points out that it has two different functions: it can be used to illustrate information or to create participation. (This is going to get a little complicated, so tighten your shoelaces.)

Allegories (and examples) use figurative language to *illustrate* information, but we have to possess the information in order to understand the illustration. The information comes first. Without the information, we are not able to participate in the communication event. For example, *The Pilgrim's Progress* is a famous allegory, but a reader would have to possess some information about the Christian life to really understand the message that John Bunyan was trying to communicate. I have heard that *Gulliver's Travels* is a political allegory, but I know so little about English politics in the late 1600s that I do not understand the allegory. (To me it is just a story about a guy on a really odd trip.) Because I do not have the information necessary to understand the allegory, I cannot participate in Jonathan Swift's communication event. Lack of information precludes participation.

In contrast, a metaphor uses figurative language to *create* participation. When figurative language is used this way, the participation precedes the information. When Jesus said, "The kingdom of heaven is like a mustard seed, which a man took and planted in his field" (Matt. 13:31), all of his listeners could immediately participate in the communication event because they knew about mustard seeds, planting, and fields. Jesus used the metaphor, the verbal comparison, to engage his listeners in the communication event. Technically, a metaphor could appear as a parable or a myth, because both use figurative language to create participation, but the "parable is a metaphor of normalcy."[1] Indeed, it is the parable's friendly aura of normalcy that invites the hearer to engage more deeply in the story than he or she might in the imaginary world provided by a myth.

Sometimes a metaphor is so powerful, it can communicate nonverbally. When the early church baptized new believers, those being baptized were asked to renounce Satan and all his works. Facing westward, the direction in which the sun went down, the candidates would renounce Satan three times. Then they would

---

1. John Dominic Crossan, *In Parables: The Challenge of the Historical Jesus* (New York: Harper & Row, 1973), 14–15.

deliberately spit three times in the direction of darkness.[2] The spitting was a symbolic (nonverbal) way to communicate complete renunciation. Everyone watching the baptism saw that symbol and participated in the communication event. Jesus did the same sort of thing when he stooped and wrote with his finger on the dusty stone of the temple floor (John 8:6) and when he put his fingers in the deaf man's ears (Mark 7:33). Symbols engage people in the communication event. During that engagement, the information encapsulated in the metaphor is conveyed.

Parables are not the kind of speech we use simply to convey information. Parables, and the metaphors that empower them, are used to affect attitudes, compel a decision, or change behavior.[3] This was a very common way to use language in the ancient Mediterranean world. Metaphor allowed a speaker to communicate more meaning than he or she could with concepts alone. Kenneth Bailey makes this point at length:

> Metaphorical language is the *primary* language, which creates the meaning set forth in the discourse. The metaphor says *more* than the conceptual frame. The conceptual interpretive language is important yet secondary. The reader of Is. 53:7–8 knows that the lamb is unjustly treated and that it is silent. Thoughtful contemplation on this "parable of the lamb before its killer and shearer" has for centuries taken readers into great depths of meaning that reach far beyond the interpretation that encases the parable.[4]

Bailey employs a musical reference to illustrate how metaphors can say more than conceptual language can convey:

2. Timothy George, "Is Christ Divided?" *Christianity Today,* July 2005, 32.
3. Robert H. Stein, *An Introduction to the Parables of Jesus* (Philadelphia: Westminster, 1981), 66.
4. Kenneth E. Bailey, *Finding the Lost: Cultural Keys to Luke 15* (St. Louis: Concordia, 1992), 18.

Beethoven's Ninth Symphony rises to its climax in the final movement. In that movement the instruments try again and again to carry the freight of the meaning the composer intends. The strings strain and strain and are unable to succeed. Finally resolution appears, as the symphony breaks into human voices with language in the great "Ode to Joy." In like manner Isaiah begins with conceptual language and then breaks into metaphor as a form of language with a higher potential for the creation of meaning.[5]

Bailey does not resist the idea that a metaphor can be "squeezed" and concepts extracted, but he rightly insists that the metaphor is always larger and more comprehensive than what is extracted.

Put it another way, we could note a person who buys an orange, takes it home and squeezes the juice into a glass for breakfast. The methodology of squeezing the orange assists the person in putting the content of the orange into a form that is easily accessible to the purchaser. Well and good. But the full orange (before squeezing) is a greater reality than the small glass of juice, however appropriate the squeezing of the orange may be. Even so, biblical metaphors can be "squeezed" and concepts extracted. To do so is not a violation of the metaphor. It is a useful exercise of great antiquity, . . . but the end result is less, not more, than the metaphor. The condensation of the meaning of the metaphor into concept catches a part, but not all, of the metaphor. The metaphor speaks to us on a deeper level. . . . [It] combines a concrete base in the physical world that can be seen and touched and felt with an unseen spiritual reality. Thus the metaphor speaks to the whole person in a way that concept does not.[6]

---

5. Ibid., 18.
6. Ibid., 18–19.

Parables are used when we want to speak to the whole person and affect attitude, compel a decision, or encourage a change in behavior. To accomplish this, they often employ a standard set of elements. We want to look at those elements next.

The Elements of a Parable

Most parables have a broad, two-part structure: the story itself (*mashal*) and the explanation (*nimshal*).[7] Although a *mashal* might be "squeezed" to extract any number of different *nimshalim*, usually there is one *nimshal* that becomes attached and becomes seen as the main lesson. For example, the *mashal* of the Good Samaritan has an attached *nimshal* about neighbors. The *mashal* of the Unrighteous Judge has an attached *nimshal* about persistence in prayer.

Harvey McArthur and Robert Johnston conducted a comprehensive study of early rabbinic parables and reported that a *mashal* was often introduced with an explicit label ("The kingdom is like . . ." or "He told them a parable . . .") or an abbreviated label ("It is like unto . . .") and will, in its most complete form, have the following five parts:

1. Illustrand—the point being illustrated. This is not structurally part of the parable, but it provides the context and is usually the reason why the parable was told.
2. Introductory formula—the explicit label (noted above) or a rhetorical question: "Unto what is the matter like?"
3. The parable proper—the story itself.
4. Application—often the rabbis attached an explicit interpretation or application; usually introduced by the Hebrew word *kak* (even so; likewise).
5. Scriptural quotation—often introduced by the formula "as it is said" or "as it is written."

---

7. David B. Gowler, *What Are They Saying About the Parables?* (Mahwah, NJ: Paulist, 2000), 48.

"The full structural pattern just described is both typical and common, but frequently one or more of these elements is lacking."[8]

The parables of Jesus predate the standardization of this pattern, so very few of his parables conform fully; however they obviously come from the same cultural milieu.[9] Craig Evans provides a helpful summary:

> Our survey of early Jewish parables makes it clear that Jesus' parables are right at home in first-century Jewish Palestine. In most respects Jesus' parables are not unique. Their emphasis on the kingdom of God roughly parallels the rabbis' emphasis on God as king, though with important differences. Jesus' parables are similar in form. . . . They are about the same length as the rabbinic parables. Sometimes allegorical features are present. Kings, banquets, travels, and business dealings are common themes. Parables are usually used to illustrate or defend an interpretation of Scripture or a point of doctrine. . . . The Old Testament parables and related materials probably supplied the basic forms and contents out of which Jesus and his contemporaries fashioned their parables.[10]

The Old Testament parables and related materials supplied the forms, because Jesus lived in a cultural environment shaped by those Scriptures.

8. Harvey K. McArthur and Robert M. Johnston, *They Also Taught in Parables* (Grand Rapids: Zondervan, 1990), 99.
9. The whole question of the relationship between the parables of Jesus and the parables of the rabbis has provoked a wealth of discussion. For major treatments of this issue, with excellent surveys of the related literature, see the cited works by Brad H. Young, *Jesus and His Jewish Parables: Rediscovering the Roots of Jesus' Teaching* (Mahwah, NJ: Paulist, 1989); and Harvey K. McArthur and Robert M. Johnston, *They Also Taught in Parables*.
10. Craig A. Evans, "Parables in Early Judaism," in *The Challenge of Jesus' Parables*, ed. Richard N. Longenecker (Grand Rapids: Eerdmans, 2000), 72–73.

The stories Jesus told were similar, but not identical, to the ones told by the rabbis who followed him. Arland Hultgren identifies six things that mark the parables of Jesus as unique and original:

- The audience was addressed directly.
- The story (*mashal*) is prominent and usually stands alone. The attached *nimshal* is minimal, thus providing much room for individual interpretation and application.
- The stories do not require previous learning; common life experience provides all that is necessary to understand.
- In their portrayal of God, "they are thoroughly theological."
- Many have an unexpected ending, "an element of surprise."
- They capture, combine, and make use of the major Jewish traditions of wisdom and eschatology.[11]

These are all important differences; however, the most important difference between the parables of Jesus and the parables told by the rabbis is one of focus. Rabbinic parables were almost always used to clarify a teaching point or explain the sense of a biblical passage. David Gowler cites evidence gathered by David Stern that suggests the rabbis initially used parables in a variety of contexts (recitations at banquets, as responses to polemical questions and challenges, or as a means of expression during a time of public crisis), but eventually they became convinced that the proper use of parable was during the delivery of the sermon in the synagogue and the study of the Torah in the academy.[12] Jesus told similar stories, but his parables were not focused on explaining a sermon or illustrating a lesson—they *were* the sermon; they *were* the lesson.

Another way to understand this difference in approach is to

---

11. Arland J. Hultgren, *The Parables of Jesus: A Commentary* (Grand Rapids: Eerdmans, 2000), 8–10.
12. Gowler, *What Are They Saying About the Parables?* 53.

remember the two functions of figurative language. The rabbis used parables in line with the first function—to illustrate truth. Jesus used parables in line with the second function—to create participation. McArthur and Johnston highlight this difference:

> While the rabbinic parables seek to reinforce conventional values, those of Jesus tend to undermine or invert them. The parables of the Rabbis seek to resolve perplexities but those of Jesus create them. The parables of the Rabbis intend to make life and thought smoother, but those of Jesus make them harder. It is the upsetting quality of the typical gospel parable that provided the clearest contrast with that of the rabbinic literature. Jesus the parabler was a subversive.[13]

Jesus was trying to seek and save those who were lost and set free those who were held captive by the Evil One—more than mere illustration was needed.

How to Interpret Parables

Scholars revel in complex discussions about how the metaphorical language of the parables is to be understood. Without joining that debate, we could note, with Kenneth Bailey, that there are always at least four levels in a parable:

> The first is the entertaining story. "Children of all ages" quickly catch this aspect of the parable. A second level is that of ethics. The parable sets forth ethical patterns to be imitated or avoided. The third is theology. The parable usually contains a revelation of the secrets of the kingdom of God. Finally, the parable *may* exhibit Christology. Jesus may be saying something about himself.[14]

---

13. McArthur and Johnston, *They Also Taught in Parables*, 114.
14. Bailey, *Finding the Lost*, 50.

From the beginning, there was more to the parables than the obvious. Indeed, Jesus seemed to use this more-than-the-obvious aspect to intentionally disarm his listeners and penetrate their defenses. This insight about disarming and persuading helps us understand a perplexing conversation that Jesus had with his disciples about parables. Here is how Matthew recorded it:

> The disciples came to him and asked, "Why do you speak to the people in parables?"
>
> He replied, "The knowledge of the secrets of the kingdom of heaven has been given to you, but not to them. Whoever has will be given more, and he will have an abundance. Whoever does not have, even what he has will be taken from him. This is why I speak to them in parables:
>
> > "Though seeing, they do not see;
> > > though hearing, they do not hear or understand.
>
> In them is fulfilled the prophecy of Isaiah:
>
> > "'You will be ever hearing but never understanding;
> > > you will be ever seeing but never perceiving.
> > For this people's heart has become calloused;
> > > they hardly hear with their ears,
> > > and they have closed their eyes.
> > Otherwise they might see with their eyes,
> > > hear with their ears,
> > > understand with their hearts
> > and turn, and I would heal them.'
>
> But blessed are your eyes because they see, and your ears because they hear. For I tell you the truth, many prophets and righteous men longed to see what you see but did not see it, and to hear what you hear but did not hear it." (Matt. 13:10–17)

Perhaps Jesus was explaining that he spoke in parables because parables were capable of piercing calloused hearts, penetrating dull ears, and opening closed eyes. Perhaps the disciples were blessed, not because they could discern some "secret" level of meaning, but because they did not suffer from those disabilities.

The passage Jesus cited from Isaiah seems to support this interpretation. The prophet seems to promise that if the people's impediments could be overcome—if the people could see, hear, and understand—they could be healed.

He said, "Go and tell this people:

> "'Be ever hearing, but never understanding;
>   be ever seeing, but never perceiving.'
> Make the heart of this people calloused;
>   make their ears dull
>   and close their eyes.
> Otherwise they might see with their eyes,
>   hear with their ears,
>   understand with their hearts,
> and turn and be healed."
>
> (Isa. 6:9–10)

Jesus' mission was to seek and save those who were lost. He came to heal the blind and the deaf and to bring understanding. I think he was explaining that parables were an extremely effective way of doing that. Parables were a way to make people open their ears and their eyes. Parables were a way to pierce calloused hearts.

As powerful as parables are, it is important to remember that it was not the form itself that changed lives.

It is not a literary form *per se* that transforms hearers or produces in them a response. Rather, such effects are the result of a combination of (1) the persuasive and disarming nature of the literary form, (2) the truth of the divine message encapsulated in that form, (3) the convicting work of God's Spirit working through the particular vehicle and message, and (4) a human response. All of these factors in combination bring about transformation and "event." And of these factors, the literary form must be judged to be the most dispensable.[15]

A parable may be powerful, but only God's truth and the Holy Spirit can change lives.

Looking Back

Jesus used parables to create participation, to challenge viewpoints, and to press for change. He used standard elements in unique ways. Because Jesus' audience was familiar with this metaphorical approach, the Holy Spirit could use this form to draw many to salvation. In the next chapter, we will look at when ministry stories were used most effectively.

---

15.   Robert H. Stein, "The Genre of the Parables," in *The Challenge of Jesus' Parables,* ed. Richard N. Longenecker (Grand Rapids: Eerdmans, 2000), 40.

CHAPTER SIX

When a Story Is the Best Response

If history were taught in the form of stories, it would never be forgotten.

—RUDYARD KIPLING

WHENEVER WE FACE A COMMUNICATION challenge, telling a story is a good option, and sometimes it is the very best option. My research suggests that there are five situations in which a ministry story (or parable) may be the very best way to respond. Stories are an effective way to

- explore a range of plausible endings.
- reveal worlds that are otherwise closed.
- clarify or reinforce role expectations.
- provide key insights.
- challenge beliefs or behaviors.

In this chapter, I will comment briefly on each of these situations and provide examples of how Jesus and other leaders used stories in each of these five ways. I should acknowledge that by my count Jesus told at least forty-six parables, and sorting them into only five categories cannot help but be a bit arbitrary. Obviously, some of his stories could fit into several categories, and the greatest ones (like the Good Samaritan or the Lost Son) could be seen as fitting into all five categories. Nevertheless, by looking at the parables according to these five categories, we can gain some insight into when Jesus thought a story was the best response and what sort of story he told in that situation. For space reasons, I will simply list the references where these parables are found.

Stories Explore a Range of Plausible Endings

A story can explore a range of plausible endings and expose the likely results of different choices. In the parable of the Sower, Jesus explores four different endings, depending on what sort of soil the seed fell into. In the parable of the Wise and Foolish Builders, Jesus explores two different endings, depending on whether the house was built on sand or rock. Here are the parables Jesus told to explore plausible endings:

Title	Passages
The Barren Fig Tree	Luke 13:6–9
The Narrow and Wide Gates	Matthew 7:13–14
The Sower	Matthew 13:3–23; Mark 4:2–20; Luke 8:4–15
The Ten Minas	Luke 19:11–27
The Two Debtors	Luke 7:41–43
The Two Sons	Matthew 21:28–31
The Wedding Banquet	Matthew 22:1–14; Luke 14:16–24
The Wise and Foolish Builders	Matthew 7:24–27; Luke 6:47–49

In each of these parables, the main point seems to be to show how different choices lead to different ends.

Here is a story the rabbis told to explain why two enemies might unite:

It is like two dogs that were with a sheep herd and were continually quarreling. Then a wolf came to steal a lamb from the flock, and one of the dogs started to attack him. The other dog said to himself: If I don't go to his assistance now, then the wolf will kill him and later attack and kill me. So the two made peace and together attacked the wolf.[1]

Technically, this story is a fable (because the central figures are animals acting like people) that explores a range of possible outcomes. Continued quarreling might produce mutual destruction. Peace might produce success. Each ending is plausible, and the story helps expose the consequences of the different choices. Stories are an effective way to explore various plausible endings.

Stories Reveal Worlds That Are Otherwise Closed

Stories are a wonderful way to reveal worlds that are otherwise beyond our natural experience. Jesus often used parables to reveal something about God the Father, the kingdom of heaven, or the final judgment. In each case, the parable helps us understand a truth about a world that would otherwise be closed to us. Here are the parables that Jesus told to reveal hidden things:

Title	Passages
The Asking Son	Matthew 7:9–10; Luke 11:11–12
The Budding Fig Tree	Matthew 24:32; Mark 13:28; Luke 21:29–30
The Empty House	Matthew 12:43–45; Luke 11:24–26
The Friend at Midnight	Luke 11:5–8
The Growing Seed	Mark 4:26–29
The Lost Coin	Luke 15:8–10
The Lost Sheep	Matthew 18:12–14; Luke 15:3–7
The Mustard Seed	Matthew 13:31–32; Mark 4:30–32; Luke 13:18–19
The Net	Matthew 13:47–50
The Pearl	Matthew 13:45–46

---

1. Harvey K. McArthur and Robert M. Johnston, *They Also Taught in Parables* (Grand Rapids: Zondervan, 1990), 66.

The Rich Man and Lazarus	Luke 16:19–31
The Sheep and the Goats	Matthew 25:31–46
The Thief	Matthew 24:43–44; Luke 12:39–40
The Workers in the Vineyard	Matthew 20:1–16
The Yeast	Matthew 13:33; Luke 13:21

In each of these parables, Jesus reveals in a wonderful, memorable way something hidden about God, the kingdom, or the future.

Here is a story that a judge used to reveal the hidden motives behind his behavior.

> A judge with an exemplary record and unquestionable character came up for reelection. Most of his colleagues were confident that he would retain his seat without contest. But then, a challenger stepped forward.
>
> To everyone's surprise, this new opponent launched a vicious mudslinging campaign. Unfounded allegations of wrongdoings began to circulate about the judge. Although most people believed the criticisms were false, eyebrows were raised as seeds of doubt were planted.
>
> As the campaign progressed, the judge refused to comment on the accusations being made against him. Finally, someone asked how he planned to handle the rumors. The judge shared this wisdom:
>
> "My family used to have a dog. On nights when the moon was full, that dog would howl at the moon all night. But despite all the dog's noise, the moon continued to shine. Well, I'm going to continue to shine while my opponent makes all kinds of noise."[2]

Of course, the story does not tell us whether the judge was reelected, but it does show us the hidden world of his personal motives and inspires us to behave in a similarly honorable way.

---

2. Cited in *Bits and Pieces,* August 2003, 16–17.

Stories Clarify or Reinforce Role Expectations

A story is a powerful way to clarify or reinforce a role expectation. Jesus often used parables to describe what a disciple is expected to be and do. His expectations that a disciple would be "the light of the world" or "the salt of the earth" are presented in memorable parables. Here are parables Jesus told that help us understand role expectations:

Title	Passages
The City on a Hill	Matthew 5:14
The Defendant	Matthew 5:25–26; Luke 12:57–59
The Doctor and the Sick	Mark 2:17
The Good Samaritan	Luke 10:30–37
The Lamp and the Bushel	Matthew 5:15; Mark 4:21; Luke 11:33
The Master and the Servants	Luke 17:7–10
The Plowman	Luke 9:62
The Salt of the Earth	Matthew 5:13; Mark 9:50; Luke 14:34–35
The Servant in Authority	Matthew 24:45–51; Luke 12:42–46
The Storeroom	Matthew 13:52
The Talents	Matthew 25:14–30
The Ten Virgins	Matthew 25:1–13
The Tower Builder	Luke 14:28–30
The Weeds	Matthew 13:24–30
The Workers and the Harvest	Matthew 9:37–38; Luke 10:2

These parables clarify or reinforce the role expectations of a disciple.

Here is an example of a parable attributed to Rabbi Akiba, which he told to reinforce the importance of studying Torah.

> Once the wicked Government [i.e., the Romans] issued a decree forbidding the Jews to study and practice the Torah. Pappus b. Judah came and found R. Akiba publicly bringing gatherings together and occupying himself with Torah. He said to him: Akiba, are you not afraid of the government?
>
> He said to him: I will parable to thee a parable. Unto [tell you]

what is the matter like? It is like a fox who was walking alongside a river, and he saw fishes going in swarms from one place to another. He said to them: From what are you fleeing? They replied: From the nets cast for us by men. He said to them: Would you like to come onto the dry land so that you and I can live together in the way my ancestors lived with your ancestors? The fish said to him: Art thou the one that they call the cleverest of the animals? Thou art not clever but foolish. If we are afraid in the element in which we live, how much more in the element in which we would die.

So it is with us. If such is our condition when we sit and study Torah, of which it is written, "For that is thy life and the length of thy days" (Deut. 30:20), if we go and neglect it, how much worse off we shall be.[3]

R. Akiba clearly expects that devout Jews would continue to study Torah regardless of what the Romans decreed. The parable seems intended to clarify or reinforce a role expectation—devout Jews study Torah.

Modern-day pastors also tell stories to reinforce role expectations. I read Leith Anderson's story about "parish poker" years ago, and it has helped me to make better leadership decisions. Here, Anderson tells the story and helps us apply it.

Several years ago I was on a panel discussing leadership, and I used an analogy that caught the attention of Terry Muck, then editor of *Leadership* magazine. He asked me to write an article about it, which I did and which he published under the title "How to Win at Parish Poker" (for the record, I did not create the title). The leadership concept is valid even though the analogy seems strange.

Becoming a pastor is like joining a poker game.

---

3. Quoted in McArthur and Johnston, *They Also Taught in Parables,* 26–27.

Although I am neither a gambler nor a poker player, I know that at the beginning of a game each player has a limited number of chips to play with and must use them strategically to win.

Churches generally give new pastors 50 to 100 "chips" to get started. After that, they either gain chips or lose what they have, depending on how well they learn the catalog of rewards and penalties their church runs by (which of course, no one bothered to tell the new pastor about). For example:

Preach a good sermon	+2 chips
Preach a bad sermon	-8 chips
Visit a sick person in the hospital	+7 chips
Sick person dies (was expected to recover)	-10 chips
Sick person recovers (was expected to die)	+40 chips
Bring cookies to monthly board meeting	+2 chips
Lose temper and shout at monthly board meeting	-25 chips

This is just a sampling. The entire catalog is very large.

A friend of mine was called to pastor a conservative Midwestern church. He arrived a few weeks early to get settled before his first Sunday. On the Sunday before his first Sunday, he gave away the pulpit to another congregation (without asking permission). That cost him 2,000 chips, which meant that if he preached 1,000 consecutive good sermons (which would take roughly twenty years) he would be back to zero. He was done. He didn't have enough chips to survive.

In contrast, another pastor friend of mine forgot a funeral. While the family was waiting for him at the local funeral home, he was eating lunch with another parishioner at a local restaurant. The funeral director called the church office, but the secretary couldn't find him. (He had chosen that day to try a new restaurant.) The funeral director started down the church listings in the yellow pages until he found a willing cleric from some alien denomination who didn't know the deceased and didn't do a very good job. When my friend realized what he had done, he immediately drove to the family home to apologize (by then the deceased had already been buried). The family spokesperson said they would never forgive him. This whole story cost him about 30,000 chips. But he had been the pastor of that church for about 40 years and had millions of chips in storage.

As you can see, it takes a lot of work to accumulate enough chips to be trusted and followed. Here are some of the rules:

- Credentials (e.g., education, ordination, previous leadership positions and successes) don't count for much. Chips aren't transferable.
- Chips are easier to win and lose in a crisis.
- Some churches and other organizations are stingy with chips. Some are generous.
- Some previous leaders leave their chips behind for the new leader to use; others come back and steal the new leader's chips.
- Chips must be piled up for significant changes. Never underestimate how many chips it will take, and don't squander your chips on issues that don't really matter.
- Learn the chips' rewards and penalties by asking, but really learn from trial and error. You may be surprised. Remember the score.
- Some leaders give you their chips; some take them away when you're not looking.
- Practice Christian stewardship of all chips. They are not to be used for the leader's personal benefit (e.g., prestige, position, salary, office, vacation).

Chips are to be reinvested for the cause and the
glory of Jesus Christ.[4]

The wonderful thing about this extended metaphor is that it
continues to provoke beneficial insight into the role of a pastor
and provides practical guidance on how to make good choices. A
leader begins to evaluate every situation he or she faces in terms
of whether chips will be won or lost.

Stories Provide Key Insights

Stories often provide key insights. A story allows the listener to
step out of his or her usual frame of reference and see something
new. In a sense, all of Jesus' parables provide key insights, but
some seem to do it in especially pointed ways. Here are parables
Jesus told to provide insight:

Title	Passages
The Divided Household	Matthew 12:25–26; Mark 3:23–26; Luke 11:17–18
The Lost Son	Luke 15:11–32
The Patched Garment	Matthew 9:16; Mark 2:21; Luke 5:36
The Strong Man	Matthew 12:29

Often the insight provided is intended to deepen our understanding of spiritual realities or show us something important about
the heavenly Father.

The rabbis also told stories to provide insight into the character
of God. This parable from the Hasidic tradition seems to emphasize the gracious mercy of God.

Once, long ago, when one of the great rabbis saw a misfortune threatening Israel, he would go to a certain place
in the forest where he would light a fire and say a special
prayer. A miracle would then happen, and disaster would

---

4. Leith Anderson, *Leadership That Works* (Grand Rapids: Bethany, 1999), 187–89.

be averted. Years later when other misfortunes threatened Israel, the rabbi's disciple went to God to intercede. He returned to the same place in the forest and said, "Master of the Universe, I am not able to light the fire, but I can still say the prayer." Again, a miracle would happen. Many years later, yet another rabbi went to intercede for Israel. He would go to the place in the forest and say, "Master of the Universe, I cannot light a fire, and I do not know the prayer, but I do know the place, and it must be sufficient." And it was. The miracle happened. Finally many, many years later, misfortune threatened again. Another rabbi sat in his armchair in his study and with his head in his hands prayed. "Master of the Universe, I cannot light the fire, and I do not know the prayer. I cannot even find the place in the forest. But I can tell the story, and it must be sufficient." And it was.[5]

In its emphasis on the power and mercy of God, this story provides key insights about God.

Sometimes, simply creating a story will provide beneficial insight. Several of the stories I will share in chapter 7 did that. "Pictures" helped me to figure out what to do in a difficult counseling situation. "Jump!" helped resolve my frustration in a church conflict situation.

Using stories this way is more personal, but the insight is often therapeutic. The insight gained can then be shared with larger groups.

Stories Challenge Beliefs or Behaviors

Parables are an effective way to challenge beliefs or behaviors in a relatively safe way. The story tends to externalize the difficult issue and provide some emotional distance between the teller and

---

5. Susan M. Shaw, *Storytelling in Religious Education* (Birmingham, AL: Religious Education Press, 1999), 32–33.

the issue. The emotional distance of "using the third person" allows a person to address emotionally charged issues indirectly.

If we look in the Gospels, we see that Jesus sometimes used parables in this way. His stories often had elements that were culturally provocative (a Samaritan hero or a praying tax collector) or amazingly confrontational (playing children), but because these provocative elements were in story form, they obtained a hearing. Here are parables that Jesus told in which the aspect of confrontation seems particularly evident:

Title	Passages
The Blind Leading the Blind	Matthew 15:14; Luke 6:39
The Pharisee and the Tax Collector	Luke 18:9–14
The Playing Children	Matthew 11:16–17; Luke 7:31–32
The Rich Fool	Luke 12:16–21

In each of these stories, the point is clearly confrontational, but the parable allows the point to be made from a safe distance. This distance allows the teller to confront in a way that gives the listener room to respond.

Here is a story-poem that subtly challenges our behavior and provokes us to think about parental influence.

Mommy's Song

When I was young I heard a song,
One song, I heard no others.
I learned the words and sang along,
The song, it was my mother's.

She never told me how to sing,
She never told me why,
She simply sang the song she'd heard
When she was young as I.

Some lines were repeated.
Some lines were repeated.
Some lines were repeated.
And some of them were wise.

They were Mommy's Bible.
They were Mommy's blueprint.
They were Mommy's comfort.
But some of them were lies.

I often write my own songs now.
But more than now and then
I find the voice inside me
Singing Mommy's song again.[6]

This story-poem makes a powerful point from a safe distance, and the rhythm and rhyme make it easy to remember.

Looking Back

Stories and parables are most effective in difficult situations. They help us to explore a range of plausible endings, reveal realities that are otherwise closed to us, clarify and reinforce role expectations, provoke insights, and challenge beliefs or behavior. The indirect nature of the communication allows the teller to be very candid while retaining enough emotional distance to feel safe.

---

6. Amy Powers, "Mommy's Song." Used by permission.

CHAPTER SEVEN

Creating an Original Ministry Story

I don't know if that's the way it really happened, but I know it's true.

—BLACK ELK

IN THE BEGINNING, I SUGGESTED THAT you could think of this book as a mountain-climbing adventure. By now we have crossed the foothills, located our chosen peak, and actually begun our ascent. At this point, we are camping at the elevation where most other climbers turn around and go back. Most people are content to understand how stories work and how Jesus used them, but we want more. We want to create original ministry stories the way Jesus did. We want to climb higher, so in this chapter we'll go for the summit. Everything we have covered so far has been leading up to this chapter, where I want to show you how to create your own ministry stories. Before we make the final ascent, let me spend one paragraph in review—looking back on our trail—and a few paragraphs looking ahead, mapping the route we will use to get to the summit.

Looking back, we have seen that ministry stories, like parables, are short stories that compare one thing or situation with another. Most are intentionally a bit indirect, which allows a difficult point to be made in a safe way. Ministry stories always have a point. The point may be to explore a range of possible responses, reveal a hidden reality, reflect on a role expectation, provide some key insight, or challenge a belief, but there is always a point. Like parables, ministry stories do not provide closure; they provoke a response. They do not have to settle an issue; instead, they are content to stimulate reflection and encourage change.

Before we move ahead, we need to acknowledge that stories are an art form, and it is probably impossible to fully explain how to create art. Like any other artist, a storymaker needs to have some basic training, but step-by-step instructions seldom produce good art. When I was young, my grandmother sent me a paint-by-numbers picture of two beautiful golden retrievers. I carefully followed the instructions and painted the odd shapes printed on the board with the designated colors. When I was done, the picture looked pretty good (especially if you stood back and squinted a bit), but it was not art, and the experience did not make me an artist. In the same way, if we approach storymaking as if it were a paint-by-numbers painting, we might end up with something pretty good, but it will not be art, and we will not become better storymakers.

Instead of step-by-step instructions, I want to give you some general guidelines, suggest some places where you can find inspiration, remind you of the importance of shape and sequence, and then show you some examples. Honestly, with just that much to go on, you can create your own stories.

General Guidelines for Storymaking

An effective ministry story is short, simple, and clear, like a three-act mini-play. The opening act sets the scene, presents the situation, and introduces the main characters. The second act usually introduces the crisis, describes any conflict that results, and reveals the complications and consequences of the actions taken. In act three, the crisis is resolved or the problem is solved. Because ministry stories are short-short stories, the cast of characters must be small, the crisis must be clear, the plot must be simple, and the resolution must be quick. Let me illustrate what I mean, using the story Jesus told at the end of the Sermon on the Mount.

> Therefore everyone who hears these words of mine and puts them into practice is like a wise man who built his house on the rock. The rain came down, the streams rose, and the winds blew and beat against that house; yet it did not fall, because it had its foundation on the rock. But everyone who hears these words of mine and does not put them into practice is like a foolish man who built his house on sand. The rain came down, the streams rose, and the winds blew and beat against that house, and it fell with a great crash. (Matt. 7:24–27)

Notice that the cast is small: only two builders. The cast in any ministry story can typically be as small as two people or two groups, because we need only enough participants to produce a comparison.

The situation is not complicated: the two men each build a house. The only difference is where they build—either on rock or on sand. The details and descriptions are minimal.

The plot advances with action, and the crisis quickly becomes clear: there is a storm that brings rain, rising water, and wind. This turn of events provides an element of the unexpected and captures and retains our attention. We can see the predicament in our mind's eye, and we want to know what will happen to the houses.

The resolution is swift—the house on the rock withstands the storm; the house on the sand collapses—and the explanation and summation are minimal. All we have by way of explanation is that the one house stood because its foundation was on the rock.

This story is so simple it is elegant, and that is part of its power. This is the sort of story that we hear once and remember forever.

Let me make one final, somewhat technical, but important point. If you tell a story from a third-person perspective, you have more freedom. As philosophy professor Lynne Tirrell points out, "First person narrators, who are characters within their own stories, are usually limited to a fallible human perspective on the events of the story."[1] A third-person narrator can tell the story as if he or she knows everything. The third-person perspective provides more freedom to make your point.

So, to summarize the general guidelines, keep your story short, three-part simple, and tell it from a third-person perspective. Advance the plot with action; show, don't tell.

Places to Find Inspiration

The process of creating an original ministry story begins when we face a challenging situation and realize that we can respond with a story. Our first impulse might be to respond to the challenge with a principle or a platitude, but the realization that we could use a story produces a sort of internal paradigm shift. The realization immediately leads to a consideration of what story we should tell.

An original ministry story begins with a clear understanding of the point we want to make and a flash of inspiration. I call this flash of inspiration a *story seed*. *Story seeds* are the ideas, the images, or the insights from which a story grows. *Story seeds* can be found almost anywhere, but there are four particularly fruitful places: existing stories, expanded stories, what-if stories, and connected stories.

Existing Stories

A new story can grow from an existing story. The simplest form simply substitutes new ideas into an old story. George Barna does this in his book *A Fish Out of Water* and calls it a "faux parable."

---

1. Lynne Tirrell, "Storytelling and Moral Agency," *Journal of Aesthetics and Art Criticism* 48, no. 2 (1990): 118.

As Jesus started on his way, a man ran up to him and fell on his knees.

"Good teacher," he asked. "What must I do to be a great leader who is Christian?"

"Why do you call me good?" Jesus answered. "No one is good except God alone. You know the requirements: cast God's vision, motivate people to pursue it, mobilize them efficiently, strategically guide their efforts, and develop the resources necessary to fulfill the vision."

"Teacher," he declared, "all these I have done since I have been a leader."

Jesus looked at him and loved him. "One thing you lack," he said. "Change your philosophy of leadership from achieving success to being obedient, and you will truly be useful to your Father in heaven."

At that the man's face fell. He went away because he had great success in leadership.

Jesus looked around and said to his disciples, "How hard it is for the leaders of this world to lead in ways that honor God."[2]

I did a similar thing when I preached a sermon series on the parables in Luke. I introduced the parable of the Two Sons (Luke 15:11–32) with the following story:

Once upon a time there was a businessman who had two sons. The businessman owned a factory that produced fine wood furniture. The business was very successful and provided employment for his sons and many others.

One day the younger son came up to his father and said, "Old Man, I know that when you die I will get control of part of this business, and I am tired of waiting. I want my share now."

---

2. George Barna, *A Fish Out of Water* (Nashville: Integrity, 2002), 189.

Now you might expect the father to deck the boy, but instead he saw his lawyer and transferred all the assets of the business to his two sons.

The younger son immediately hired an auctioneer and liquidated his share. He took the money and flew to Las Vegas, rented a condo, and began to host a continuous series of parties—lots of wine, women, and rock music.

Eventually the money ran out and things began to get bad. A gas shortage and an airline strike caused a severe economic depression in Nevada; even the casinos had to lay people off. The young man became desperate. His money was all gone, there were no jobs to be had, he was sleeping on the street, and he was very hungry.

Eventually he became so desperate that he went to the county hospital and refused to leave until they gave him a job emptying bedpans for terminally ill AIDS patients. Because he was so desperate, they did not even pay him minimum wage, so he could not afford much to eat. During the day, he found himself longing for the food the dying patients left on their lunch trays.

One day he came to his senses and said to himself, "Boy, even the second shift janitors in my father's factory have plenty to eat, and I am starving to death. I am going to go home and admit to my father that I was wrong. I know I have forfeited the privilege of being treated as his son, but I will ask him to at least let me work for him in the factory. Maybe if I work hard I can earn enough to pay back all the money I wasted." So the boy left the hospital and began to hitchhike home.

When he finally arrived in his hometown, he walked up to the gate of his father's plant. He was about to ask the security guard to page his father when he saw his father running across the parking lot toward him. His father grabbed him and right there in front of the entire workforce hugged him and kissed him over and over.

The son was overwhelmed with this public demonstration of love and suddenly realized that his plan to repay his father was foolish. There was no way he could ever repay his father for this sort of love; all he could do was admit his sin and confess his unworthiness. So he did.

His father then turned to the security guard and said, "Hurry, go to my office and bring me my jacket and my hard hat. Put them on my son here. And get him my cell phone. So they dressed the son with the jacket and the hard hat and the cell phone. Then the father said, "Call the caterer! I want enough barbecue for the entire plant, with all the fixings! Hire a band! Call in the second shift! Give everybody the rest of the day off! My son was gone and now he is back—we are going to have a party!"

As soon as the food arrived, the band began to play, and they all began to celebrate because the son that was as good as dead had come home safely.

Meanwhile, the older son, who was away dealing with some vendors, drove up in his pickup. He saw the crowd and heard the band and saw the usual bunch of little kids milling around in front of the gate. He pulled one of the kids aside and said, "What is going on here?" The kid told him that his brother who was gone had returned and that his father was throwing a party to celebrate. The older son was so angry that he would not even drive into the plant.

But his father had been watching and hurried out of the gate and urged him to join the celebration. Instead the older son exploded and right in front of everybody said, "Look! I've been slaving for you for all these years, and I've always done what you told me to. You have never given me enough to have a party at McDonalds with a few friends. Now this worthless son of yours, who wasted all your money on whores in Las Vegas, returns, and you throw a party for everybody at company expense."

Instead of decking the boy, the father simply said, "My precious son, you have always been here with me. Everything I have is yours. We have to celebrate your brother's return. He was as good as dead, and now he is alive again. Come on, join the party."

These modernized parables are the simplest stories to create because they are simply replicating work that has already been done. They are occasionally interesting as novelties and can help provoke insight by dressing the basic story up in twenty-first-century attire, but they are not really very engaging. Our familiarity with the original story makes the reproduction too obvious. Most of the energy generated by this sort of story is dissipated because the audience is distracted by comparing the two versions and therefore misses the point.

Expanded Stories

Sometimes a new story can grow as an expansion of an existing story. For example, if we added another pig to the story of "The Three Little Pigs," we would have a different story. Another way to expand a story is to continue it past the traditional ending. Susan Shaw cites several published stories, such as *The Frog Prince, Continued,* in which the Frog Prince has to deal with the realities of marriage, and everything is not so happily ever after. This sort of story is interesting because it starts somewhere familiar and ends somewhere entirely new.

Bible stories can sometimes be successfully expanded. Suppose, for example, we continued the story of the Wise and Foolish Builders and told what happened after the storm. Suppose the foolish man filed for federal disaster relief and rebuilt his house in the same place. Or suppose he moved. This sort of expansion works best when the audience is very familiar with the original story. Any expansion of a biblical story should be done cautiously and respectfully, because we do not want to inadvertently give the impression that we are adding to Scripture (cf. Rev. 22:18).

What-if Stories

Marshall Shelley believes *what-if* stories are the easiest to tell, because no research is needed, just some imagination. The story seed is to imagine an unusual situation and then think of what might happen if that situation were true. Here are some of Shelley's examples:

1. What would happen if elephants could fly?
2. What would happen if you lived underwater?
3. What would happen if your nose grew every time you got angry?
4. What would happen if a train decided it did not want to run on the tracks?[3]

Shelley points out that each of these is a potential story—actually several stories, because each situation could be told from more than one perspective. For example, the story of "what would happen if your nose grew every time you got angry" could be told from the angry person's perspective, his wife's perspective, his coworker's perspective, and his doctor's perspective, as well as many more.

This type of story seed is very fruitful for pastors, who can think of many *what-if* situations from their ministry.

- What if the amount of the offering we gave were displayed on our foreheads?
- What if emotional wounds bled?
- What if a Christian took off his armor in the middle of a battle?
- What if every critical remark left a scar?
- What if couples became conjoined twins when they married?

---

3.   Marshall Shelley, *Telling Stories to Children* (Batavia, IL: Lion, 1990), 61.

- What if there were only one kind of music?
- What if a wife were fed nothing but leftovers?

As we ponder these situations, interesting stories begin to grow.

Connected Stories

Sometimes, a new story will grow from bits of several stories that are connected or combined. In the midst of the Bill Clinton–Monica Lewinsky scandal, I did a first-person narrative sermon about King David and Bathsheba from the perspective of King David's spin doctor. The combination of a current events story and an ancient biblical story produced a powerful lesson on truth telling. The same thing can be done in parable form. Suppose the Prodigal Son worked for the Good Samaritan in the far country. Or, suppose the older son met the recovering man-who-fell-among-thieves. A combined story allows the truths of the original stories to intermingle and reveal new truth.

Shape and Sequence

Good stories can grow from any of these *story seeds*; but, like literal seeds, they need to be planted in a good place and cultivated. We cultivate *story seeds* by giving them shape and sequence. Shape and sequence help *story seeds* grow into fruitful ministry stories.

Story seeds begin to grow and take shape as we visualize a particular event or situation. Here we need to be as specific and vivid as possible, because the clearer the situation becomes to us, the easier it will be to describe it to others.

Suppose we take the story seed, "What if a wife were fed nothing but leftovers?" and try to visualize the situation. How tall is that lady? What color is her hair? Is she thin or heavy? What sort of hairstyle does she have? Does she wear perfume? Are her clothes stylish or frumpy? New or old? Store-bought or homemade? Does she have children? What does she feed them? Who cooks the food she doesn't get? How do the others get it first? Do others know that all she gets are the leftovers? What does she say to her husband about the leftovers? Stories take shape in the concrete details; blonde hair, red dress, twin girls, roast beef, and Tupperware. As we visualize the details of the situation, the story takes shape.

Once the image is clear in our minds, we need to connect emotionally to the situation. There are four basic emotions: joy, anger, sadness, and fear. We need to clarify which are present in our story. Can you empathize with the wife? Think back to the last time you were served leftovers. How did it make you feel? Think about how you felt in similar situations—wearing your brother's hand-me-downs, buying shoes at Goodwill, being chosen last during recess. Maybe there are some good emotions attached to leftovers, the last slice of a favorite pie, the last helping of Mom's meatloaf, the last piece of double pepperoni pizza. Do those apply to this story? If all you ever got were leftovers, how would you feel?

Once the emotion is clear, we need to imagine actions that will reveal these emotions. If we were watching the wife with her leftovers, what would we see? Would she sit stiffly at the table and poke at her food? Would she sigh and push her plate away? Would she eat quickly and ask to be excused? Would she look at her food and wipe tears from her eyes? Would she push back from the table and sweep her plate onto the floor? What would she do? How would her emotions be revealed? The meaning is revealed in the actions.

When the situation is clear and the emotions are identified, we need to show what happens next. The basic structure of any story is a sequence of problem/solution cycles. This sequencing is what carries the plot forward. For example, suppose the wife sweeps her plate onto the floor. *What happens next?* How do the others at the table respond? What does her husband do? Suppose the wife sits at the table and quietly begins to weep. What happens next? These cycles of problem and solution continue until the desired level of tension has been attained. We are then ready to provide a resolution.

The resolution is the final part of the story. This is where the point of the story becomes most obvious. In Jesus' story of the Good Samaritan, after the priest and the Levite pass by, the story resolves with the Samaritan stopping to help the poor traveler. The resolution doesn't necessarily provide closure, but it does need to resolve the tension. Resolution is what makes the situation into a story. Eventually, the husband is going to have to do something about what his wife is eating. What he does will reveal the point of the parable. If he repents and starts letting his wife have the first helping—that is one story. If he becomes angry at her ungrateful spirit—that is another story. If he ignores her feelings and does nothing at all—that is a third story. Each of these stories would convey a powerful point, but they would be different points.

We help a story seed take shape and grow when we visualize the situation and see the details. Once the details are clear, we connect with the emotions. With the details and the emotions, we show what happens, and then what happens after that. Finally, we show how the situation is resolved, and the point becomes clear.

Twenty Examples

Good advice is wonderful, but most of us learn best from an example or two. In this section, I will show you some ministry stories I created for typical ministry situations I have faced. The first ten deal with situations you might face in a typical church or ministry. The second ten were created for use in counseling situations. The counseling stories tend to be a bit longer and a bit darker.

For each story, I will explain the precipitating situation and then tell the story. After each story, there will be an analysis section in which I will discuss the story seed I started with and the point I was trying to make (if it is not obvious). In the analysis section, I will also reflect on some of the occasions when I have used the story, and the results.

One final thing, I did *not* create these stories on the spur of the moment. Usually, I would face the situation and do the best I

could, but later I would think about how I could have done better. Sometimes, I felt a story would have been effective, so I began
working on one. When it was ready, I had it in reserve for the
next time I faced a similar situation. There is no way to know for
sure, but I think Jesus might have done the same sort of thing. He
might have had a run-in with a Pharisee about neighbors (which
is not recorded in the Gospels) and then created that wonderful
Good Samaritan story for "the next time." Most of my stories were
crafted over a period of time; maybe his were too. If the "when" of
the story's creation is significant, I have noted that.

Example 1: Not Your Wool

Situation

In every church, there are people who do not participate. Some
are lazy, some are uncommitted, some are worn out, and some are
selfish. Pastors are familiar with all of these types. But sometimes
a person in the church does not participate for another reason—a
good reason. Here is the ministry story:

> It was shearing time. The shepherd was excited. Shearing
> time was when all the hard work paid off. The reward for
> all the green pastures, still waters, and constant vigilance
> day and night was the abundant wool that clung to ev-
> ery surface of the sheep. Bales of wool testified to healthy
> sheep and faithful shepherds. The shepherd could not
> wait to present an abundance of wool to his master.
>
> Of course, shearing time was also hard work. Sheep do
> not volunteer to be sheared. The shepherd had to care-
> fully gather them, hold them tightly, and relieve them of
> their surplus. There was dodging and crying and occa-
> sional pain, but even the sheep seemed happier when it
> was over.
>
> However, every year there were some sheep that could
> not be sheared. These could not be overlooked. For the
> shepherd, the math was clear—ninety and nine were not

enough if one was missing. The sheep that could not be sheared had to be accounted for.

The shepherd knew that some sheep hid deep in the wilderness, risking everything to avoid shearing. Some were so sparse that for their own good, nothing could be taken. Some were already shorn.

"What of them?" the shepherd asked his master. "Are they my sheep? Have we been robbed? Why are they already shorn?"

The master replied, "They are my sheep. I have given you the responsibility—but I have given their wool to others."

Analysis

The story seed was the realization that sheep live to be sheared. Wool is how sheep pay for their expenses. Wool is what the owner expects to get from a sheep. This parable is intended to encourage shepherds to diligently shear the sheep periodically. It is also intended to remind shepherds that the "wool" does not belong to us; it belongs to the Master. If he directs a bagful to this mission or that ministry, we should not be jealous.

Example 2: All You See

Situation

Almost every church has a certain number of people who join for financial benefit. Some of these are the economically distressed who want financial assistance, some are businessmen who want clients, some are in pyramid sales organizations, and others are missionaries who want support. Unfortunately, if their focus is on money, they miss the real treasure of the church. Here is the story:

A man joined a church and looked around. He did not see all the friendly faces. He did not notice the happy children. He did not notice the clean facility or the neat bulletin. He did not even notice the sad eyes that went home encouraged.

All this man saw were the wallets, brown ones, black ones, leather and vinyl, in purses and in pants, and a few in coats. All he saw in church were the wallets.

Here is the question: if all he saw were wallets, whom did he serve?

Analysis

The story seed here came from asking myself what these people really wanted from the church. It seems that what they really wanted was money, not relationships. This parable was written to rebuke their focus on money. Closing with a pointed rhetorical question was intended to provoke them to remember Matthew 6:24 or Luke 16:13.

Example 3: The Tree

Situation

Sometimes a person or a church does something that attracts God's judgment. When people reminisce, they remember the storm, they remember the strike, but they may not characterize it as a mortal blow. Here is the story:

Imagine with me that it is one of those sultry summer afternoons. Your skin is moist from the heat, your clothes feel sticky, and the breeze is too halfhearted to provide much cooling.

Nearby is a great tree. Sunshine, soil, and years have made it tall and proud. Many have found comfort in the shade of this great tree, and you join them, pondering the simple, elemental joy of sitting in the shade of a great tree on a hot day.

Off on the horizon, you notice a darkening. There is a piling up of clouds, and the erratic wind straightens and begins to blow more seriously. The sky takes on the ominous shade of a deep bruise. Occasionally, there is a gust that makes all the leaves align. The tree sways but does not bow its head—too tall, too old, too proud.

Suddenly, the wind dies down, but the clouds are accelerating. Then there is a deafening crack, and for a split second every small detail of the tree is illuminated with heavenly light. In that instant, the great tree is struck, riven, wounded, as the fire of God finds the dirt.

The storm moves away. The tree stands for years and years. Still, little by little, year-by-year, it is less lush. It still stands tall and proud, but each storm claims another branch. The shade is not as deep or as wide.

Now imagine another sultry afternoon. Off on the horizon there is a darkening. There is a piling up of clouds, and the erratic wind straightens and begins to blow more seriously. The clouds sweep overhead, the afternoon darkens, and the sky takes on an ominous shade. But even before the main body of the storm can arrive, in the midst of an ordinary gust, there comes another crack—this time from the tree—a crack and a twisting, tearing sound as the huge tree topples to the ground. It lies there, massively broken and enormously sad.

Here is the question: we know when it fell, but when did it die?

Analysis

The story seed here was from a literal tree. One afternoon, it fell, and only then did we notice that it had been dying for years. Some churches are like that—they fall on our watch, but they have been dying for years. Some people are like that—they fail under our care, but they have been dying for years. Sometimes, judgment is only obvious years later.

Example 4: Can't Won't Jane

Situation

A while back, we were having a problem with children making too many bathroom runs during services. I wanted to address this in a gentle, friendly way, so I came up with this story:

> Once upon a time, there was a little girl with an awful name. She was a very nice little girl with pretty hair and cool clothes. She had lots of friends, but her name was embarrassing.
>
> Her name was Can't Hold It, because—well, she can't hold it. When she goes out to play with her friends, she can play for only ten minutes because she can't hold it any longer than that. When she goes to the mall, she can shop for only ten minutes because she can't hold it any longer than that. When she goes to the zoo, she only sees the seals, because they are right in front of the restrooms. She simply can't hold it.
>
> Her parents took her to the doctor, but the doctor said there was nothing physically wrong with the girl. According to the doctor, she could hold it but she just wouldn't. The doctor said her name should be Won't Hold It.
>
> One Sunday she went to a new church with her family, and it was so-o-o embarrassing. The service started, and she sang a few songs, then she had to go. "Mom," she said, "I can't hold it." So she went. When she came back there was testimony time and a prayer and the offering, and she had to go again. "I can't hold it," she whispered. Then the pastor started preaching and everyone was paying attention, and she had to go again. "I can't hold it." Finally it was time for the benediction, and she had to hurry out again. "I can't hold it."
>
> After the service, all the friendly people came up and introduced themselves to her. "What is your name little

girl?" She blushed and said, "My name is Can't Hold It." They nodded and said, "Oh, of course."

On her way home, the little girl asked her mom and dad, "If I learn to hold it, can I change my name?" They smiled and said, "Oh, yes. We would be so proud."

So she did. She learned to hold it. It was not easy at first, but she did it. And they changed her name. They named her Jane. And they all lived happily ever after.

Analysis

This story seed came from the excuse we often heard from the children: "I can't hold it." The form chosen was intentionally like a children's storybook, with repetition of the main point and the unusual name. This story could easily be modified for cell phones or other distractions.

Example 5: My Favorites

Situation

In every church I have served or attended, there have been periods of tension over the style of music. Some people like hymns. Some like choruses. Some like the organ. Some like the praise band. In an effort to manage the tension, I wrote this story:

One day a man walked into a diner, sat down in the booth, and opened the menu. It was a big menu, five pages plus the insert with the specials. On the first page were all sorts of appetizers and salads. On the second page were all sorts of sandwiches, soups, and burgers. On the third page were entrées—chicken, turkey, steak, ribs, meatloaf, liver, fourteen kinds of pasta, and five kinds of fish. The top of page four had all sorts of breakfast items: eggs, omelets, hotcakes, French toast, even malted waffles. The bottom of page four listed the desserts and drinks. There was a bewildering array of food to choose from.

The man studied the menu for a moment and signaled for the waitress. "What kind of restaurant is this?" he grumbled. She looked a little puzzled and replied, "Why, we are a diner—we serve a little bit of everything." The man frowned, "Don't you know the only proper food is Italian food?" She brightened, "Sir, we have some of that. Look at page three." His frown deepened. "Not *some* Italian food, it should be *all* Italian food." The waitress looked puzzled again. "Why?" she asked in a friendly voice. "When there are so many good kinds of food, why should we serve only Italian?"

Analysis

The story seed here was to shift to something else that everyone feels passionate about—food. The story works with simple substitution. All the usual arguments for one sort of music are applied to one sort of food. The parable makes a powerful appeal for tolerance in an indirect, slightly humorous way. I tried this story on a man who was concerned about the blend of music in our services. He smiled and said, "OK, Pastor. I get it."

Example 6: Options

Situation

In every church there are members who come to the pastor for advice about a difficult situation—and then they ignore the advice and end up in the trouble they were advised to avoid. What should a pastor do in that situation? Here is the story:

The shepherd peered over the edge of the wadi. Just below him was the sheep he had been tracking, stuck in a thorn bush. The sheep bleated in an embarrassed sort of way when it saw the shepherd.

"You *should* be embarrassed, you dummy!" the shepherd grumbled. "I warned you this would happen when

we were back at the ranch. I showed you the statistics—
87.3 percent of all the sheep that wander off end up in a
wadi or in a thorn bush. Look at you. You ended up in
both!"

The shepherd climbed down and stood by the sheep.
The sheep was so thoroughly stuck that all it could do
was blink its eyes. "What am I going to do with you?" the
shepherd muttered. "What are my options?"

"Maybe I should thump you on the head or give you a
good kick in the rump? Maybe I should sit here and say,
'I told you so' ninety and nine times to remind you of
your buddies safe at home? Maybe I should wait until you
say you are sorry and ask for forgiveness?" The sheep just
blinked its eyes.

The shepherd sighed, rolled down his sleeves, put on
his gloves, and reached into the thorn bush. Slowly, carefully, he untangled the sheep. Finally, with one last tug
he pulled him out. The sheep was a mess, so exhausted
and weak that all it could do was stand there on quivering legs.

The shepherd sighed again, crouched down and lifted
the sheep onto his shoulders. Grunting a little under the
weight, he stood up and began the long walk home. He
smiled a crooked smile and asked again, "What are my
options?" Then he recited, "To seek and save those that
are lost."

Analysis

This story seed came from an interview in *Leadership* magazine.
The pastor being interviewed commented that the only good
option for dealing with a sheep in a thorn bush was to get him out.
Of course, there are other options, and the parable is intended to
surface those options and to encourage pastors to do what Jesus
did.

Example 7: Good Possums

Situation

Pastoral leadership is a challenge. Pastors know that an aggressive leadership style is seldom effective, so sometimes they are tempted to be passive. Some even see virtue in passivity. Here is the story:

> Legend has it that Romulus and Remus were raised by wolves. I was raised by possums. Legend does not say how the wolves felt, but I think the possums were disappointed with how I turned out. Here is my story.
>
> I do not know when they found me, only where. My parents were very territorial, so when Pa found me in his territory, he dragged me home. Ma's pouch was already full, so she was not enthusiastic to see Pa arrive with another baby. I've heard the story a hundred times. "Pa, what makes you think he is a possum?" she demanded. "Well," Pa mumbled, "he's actually alive but apparently dead. Isn't that what possums do?" She couldn't think of a good answer right then, so they took me in and raised me the best they knew how.
>
> Frankly, I was a burden. Their other children were weaned in one quarter, on their own in two, but I lingered. The longer I lingered, the clearer it became that I was not really a possum and would never really fit in.
>
> They taught me what they knew, and I tried to be a good possum. Real possums are solitary animals, always prowling around the edges of things, cautious and very careful. They do not handle emotions well and hate surprises. If something unexpected happens, like a headlight sweeping across their path, their first instinct is to freeze. If the light keeps coming, a good possum will keel over, loose limbed and flaccid—actually alive but apparently dead.
>
> In possum folklore, there are lots of stories of possums

that escaped danger by pretending to be dead. While I was growing up I heard them all.

I heard about Uncle Zeke. Uncle Zeke had eaten too much fermented fruit one fall evening and was staggering home, belly dragging the ground. As he came around a bush, he almost bumped into a dog. The dog growled. Uncle Zeke froze, tipped over, and lay there unmoving. The dog nudged him. Uncle Zeke flopped convincingly. The dog barked in his ear. Uncle Zeke did not even flinch. The dog nipped his long, bare tail. Uncle Zeke did not even wince. Finally the dog got bored and left. Uncle Zeke lay there a while, and then, sobered by his experience, he hurried home.

I heard about Cousin Bobbly. Cousin Bobbly got too focused on a mouse one moonlit night and nearly smacked into a fox. Cousin Bobbly immediately stiffened up, let his eyes glaze over, and collapsed with a small sigh. The fox sauntered over and poked him with a paw. When Cousin did not react, the fox rolled him over several times. Then, with a wide smile, the fox took off after the mouse that Cousin had been chasing. Cousin B-B-Bobbly stuttered for days afterward.

That is what I remember best from my childhood, all those stories of passive heroes who were only apparently dead. I grew up knowing that if I was scared, I could freeze. If I was threatened, I could flop. If I was attacked, I could just fall over and lay there, unmoving until the threat went away.

I try not to think about Pa. Pa was crossing the road one hot August night when a little deuce coupe swung around the curve. As the headlights washed over him, Pa froze, his eyes went glassy and he flopped over. The little deuce coupe kept coming, lights blazing, music blaring, horn honking. Pa didn't even twitch.

It would have made a great story, except the coupe ran

right over him. Actually, Pa did not look much different—a little flatter and wider perhaps—but if he is faking it, he fooled us all. He has not moved once since. I think he is dead. I think the apparent became actual.

I try not to think about that. I try not to ask *what if* questions. What if he had not frozen? What if he had scurried out of danger? What if passivity is not the best way to respond? Do you see why my parents were disappointed? Good possums do not ask questions like that.

Analysis

I served a church once where my predecessor had a very passive leadership style. After I had been there a while, the old-timers became weary of my more active leadership style. It was clear they wished I were passive too. This story seed came from asking, "What sort of creature makes passivity a virtue?" The story is intended to gently prod a passive pastor to think about a more active style of leadership before the apparent becomes actual.

Example 8: It's All Good

Situation

Most churches have people who are too busy to get involved in the ministry. Sometimes they attend faithfully but will not do any more than that. Here is a story for that sort of individual:

Once upon a time, there was an investor. He was hard-working, careful with details, and had nerve when he needed it. All day long he would read prospectuses, analyze reports, and look for opportunities.

Unfortunately, he always invested in something short-term. He seemed to have a knack for the immediate. Almost every day he would pass by long-term investments and find another way to spend his assets on something temporary, something transitory, something ephemeral. "It's all good," he used to say with a smile.

Sometimes people tried to convince him to invest at least a portion of his assets in something long-term. "You need to balance your portfolio," they would say. "You need something eternal." But the investor was always too busy to think about eternity. The here and now was happening so fast. "It's all good," he used to say with a smile.

That investor is gone now—he has settled into eternity. All the investments he made in the here and now are still here, not there. I wonder if he is still saying, "It's all good"?

Analysis

The story seed here comes from Jesus' exhortation to lay up treasure in heaven. This parable modernizes the concept slightly and speaks about an investor who is obviously deranged. He does it exactly wrong. The parable is intended to plant a seed of warning in anyone who may be investing his or her life the same way.

Example 9: The Gift

Situation

Some people seem to want to know all about spiritual gifts without ever using the one God gave them. Here is the story:

One Christmas, a little boy was adopted. In all of the excitement of entering his new family, he never once thought about presents.

Several weeks later, after things had settled down a little, the little boy noticed a large box, brightly wrapped in Christmas paper, sitting in the living room. It had his name on it. That night, he asked his new father about the box. His father explained that the box contained a special present for the little boy. It was his gift given to him on the day he became part of the family.

The little boy was so excited. He thanked his new father and immediately began to study all he could find about Christmas gifts. Over the next several months, he discovered there were different kinds of gifts. There were big flashy ones and little precious ones. There were happy ones and educational ones. There were practical gifts and exotic gifts. Some gifts were cash cold; others were hug warm. Everything he learned about Christmas gifts was very exciting.

As the months went by, sometimes the excitement would bubble up and the little boy would go into the living room and look at the box and wonder what was in it. He wondered, and wondered, and wondered . . . but he never opened it.

Analysis

The story seed was a what-if question: "What if a person got a present but never opened it?" The parable is intended to motivate believers to actually identify and begin to use their spiritual gifts instead of simply studying the concept. I have twice used a longer version of this story in a sermon—but it was too long. I have used this shorter version in private conversations, and it seems to be more effective.

Example 10: Soup
Situation

Usually when I preach a sermon, I sense I am bringing a message from God to his people. Sometimes I have a sense of who might benefit, but I am always surprised at who is offended. Sometimes I realize the message was not even for the one offended. Here is the story:

Once there was a waiter working in The Restaurant, serving between Cook and consumer. Cook never came out of the kitchen and rarely took orders. The consumers were used to eating the soup that was set before them with the usual sighs and smiles, compliments and complaints.

The consumers were not all alike. New consumers came in starving and ate with unseemly gusto. The regulars came in grateful for the nourishment and eager to see what Cook was cooking. Seekers were guarded, sampling the soup with tentative sips. The differences were all very familiar.

Cook had been cooking the same sort of thing for a long time: milk-based soups, broths, potage, and chowders. They were thick, nutritious, hot and smooth, but comfortable, easy soups.

One day the waiter went to the kitchen, and Cook was preparing something more robust. The vegetables were almost crisp, and the waiter could see an occasional chunk of well-done beef. He straightened up and walked a little faster. This was something new and exciting, but different—a not-so-easy soup.

The consumers were startled, but after a tentative sip or two they seemed to like it. Many asked for more and sat chewing the meat and vegetables and quietly smiling.

Sometime later, Cook was serving this not-so-easy soup again, and the waiter was carrying a second helping to a regular when he passed an old friend. The old friend stopped the waiter, scowled and motioned at the soup. "Where did you get this?" he growled. With a measuring look he declared, "This is not soup—this is pig slop!" Then with a frown he leaned over and spit in the soup.

The waiter looked at the spittle spreading over the surface of the soup. "Friend," he said, "it was not your soup. Why are you ruining it for others?" The old friend frowned more deeply and muttered stubbornly, "Bad soup—bad soup. Take it away!"

The waiter told Cook. Cook smiled and gave the waiter another bowl of soup.

Analysis

Christians should be tolerant toward what is being served. Maybe it is not for them.

Example 11: Guess Who

Situation

Sometimes life can damage people's self-image to the point that they cannot even recognize the good things about themselves. Here is the story:

> They asked her to play a get-acquainted game. Each person would have a sheet of paper taped on his or her back. On the paper would be a name—perhaps George Washington, Abraham Lincoln, Mother Teresa, or Harriet Tubman. Each person would then mingle in the crowd and ask "yes" or "no" questions in an attempt to discover the name on his or her back. Did I cross the Delaware? Did I wrestle for votes? Did I live in India? Did I run a railroad? It was a who-am-I game. She agreed to play, and they taped a name on her back.
>
> She began to ask questions: Am I a good person? Yes! Am I nice? Yes! Am I friendly? Yes! Am I smart? Yes! Am I pretty? Yes! Do I have lots of friends? Yes! Am I married? Yes! Am I a good wife? Yes! Do I have children? Yes! Am I a good mother? Yes! Do my children love me? Yes! Do I work hard? Yes! Do I respect my parents? Yes! Do I love Jesus? Yes! Do I support my church? Yes! Do I go to this church? Yes! Do you know me? Yes!
>
> By now she was very confused. She turned to the pastor, "Do I know this person?" she asked plaintively. The pastor smiled and showed her the paper taped on her back. On the paper she saw her own name.

Analysis

The story seed here was a game we played at a Sunday school

party. At the party, all the names were of famous people, but I wondered, "What if they put my own name on my back? Would I recognize myself from the good things others said about me?" I wrote the parable to encourage people to believe the good things others say about them.

Example 12: Dark Pieces

Situation

Every life is an assortment of good and bad. Usually we want to deal with the good parts and ignore the bad parts. Sometimes, however, understanding how the bad parts fit in is crucial to accomplishing what God has called us to do. Here is the story:

> He could tell it was a really large puzzle with lots of pieces, vivid colors, and intricate designs. He felt as if he had been working on the puzzle all his life, methodically picking up pieces and putting them where they belonged. Often, he would smile tightly and, with a nudge and a tap, slide another piece into place. If and when he ever got it all together, he knew the puzzle would fill the room from wall to wall.
>
> It was a challenge. The pieces were all different sizes and cut in odd, intriguing shapes. The colors were tangled and chased each other across the spectrum like children on the playground of an international school. The details were intricate and obscure.
>
> That is why he liked to work with the plain pieces. Pure and simple, easily sorted, red, blue, green, yellow, it was obvious where they fit. Unfortunately, there were not many plain pieces.
>
> He did not mind the glimmering pieces. The burnished gold, gleaming white, luminous green, and resplendent red had a furtive excitement. They were only a little intimidating and not too hard to place.
>
> He admired the pastel pieces. They looked clean and

innocent. Scrubbed beige, delicate rose, tranquil lime, and sunrise orange blended in and felt safe.

Once in a while, he would deal with something vivid, an emerald piece blazing with green fire, or a ruby piece, bright as a drop of fresh blood. Not often—it wouldn't be prudent—but once in a while was manageable.

There were some pieces he did not like—dark pieces. They were sad, melancholy pieces, and he would shift them off to the side, pile them up, and look away. Sooty, dingy, inky dark pieces. Gloomy, ominous, dreary dark pieces. Shameful, sinful, shocking dark pieces. Dishonorable, disreputable, disgraceful dark pieces. He hated the dark pieces.

One day, as he stood up to stretch, his hands absently rubbed the kink in the small of his back while his eyes roamed back and forth over the puzzle. He shifted, restless. There were scattered gaps that spoiled the sweep of color, voids that disrupted the pattern, breaches in the intricate design. He looked at those empty places and shrugged his shoulders as if to dispel a nagging sense of the familiar, a nibbling at the edge of his consciousness.

He focused on an area that was particularly bothersome. It was in a part of the puzzle where the pattern was not as dense and the colors were not so variegated. The emptiness there seemed particularly disquieting, and he frowned again at the pieces that surrounded the empty place.

With a sigh, he glanced at the pile of dark pieces. There, on the side, in the shadows, was a familiar shape. Frowning more deeply, he reached out and cautiously picked up the dark piece. In his hand it seemed so small, so innocuous, so insignificant that he almost tossed it back. Instead, with a small shrug and a grimace, he stooped down and slipped it into the empty place in the area that had been bothering him.

It fit! He rocked back on his heels and crouched staring at that dark piece. It fit and somehow blended in, like shade under a tree, like the shadow under a rock, like the dappled darkness beneath the surface of still waters. In a mystical way, the darkness enhanced the color, strengthened the pattern, and reinforced the design.

He looked over the puzzle again and with a sinking feeling realized there were more holes waiting to be filled. He took a deep, uneven breath and with a trembling hand reached for another dark piece.

Analysis

The story seed was a jigsaw puzzle and the observation that color is not a good indication of fit. Sometimes, the most unexpected colors blend to create beauty. Dark colors are necessary. I was hoping to provide encouragement to counseling clients who did not want to look at the dark parts of their lives. I also wanted to make the point that sometimes when we put the dark parts in place, the pattern of what God is doing in our lives becomes more obvious.

Example 13: Collateral Damage

Situation

When a child is raised in an abusive environment, some of the wounds inflicted leave the child disabled—unable to do what an ordinary child would do. This disability often becomes most obvious when the abusing parents are old and need care. The child may be aware of their demands but unable to respond. Here is the story:

They were old, and he knew they needed him. He could see the loneliness in their eyes. He had seen that look in the mirror. He felt responsible. It is the destiny of children to care for their parents. He could hear the distant bugle call of duty.

They felt entitled. When he was small, they had cared for him. Now that they were old it was only right that he care for them. They never asked—directly. "We don't see you much," they murmur. "We love you," they gently accuse. "We know you have your own life, but—" their voices trail away meaningfully.

He sat there hearing every word—unmoving—and felt familiar tears welling up in dry eyes. Have they forgotten? He remembered.

It was a hot afternoon. All around the house the sun blazed down on a dry and barren land. The smell of dust was in the air. He could still see the couch with its sun-faded cushions. He could still see the chair with its wide, flat, sweat-stained arms. He could still see her by the couch—flushed face, hair damp at the nape of her neck. He could still see him by the chair—silent, furious, rings of sweat under the arms of his tight, white T-shirt.

He did not hear the argument. He did not watch. He crouched, knees pulled up to his chest, arms tight around his legs—a small ball of boy unseen.

He never heard the shot. He barely felt the pain—just an almost soothing numbness as the world went still. He never moved again.

Now they are old, and he knows they need him, but all he can do is lie there—unmoving—collateral damage.

Analysis

The story seed came from watching a daughter try to care for her abusive mother, who had Alzheimer's. The daughter seemed emotionally paralyzed by her situation. She saw her duty and empathized with her mother's needs but still found herself emotionally incapable of a sincerely gracious response. The parable was intended to provide insight into the source of that ambivalence and the path to healing.

Example 14: Reflections

Situation

Some people appear unwilling to look deeply inside and try to understand the source of relational pain or dysfunction. As I puzzled about that, I came up with this story:

> Brother James once spoke of a man who looked at the face of his birth in a mirror and immediately forgot what kind of person he was. I knew a man like that.
>
> I do not mean that he never caught a glimpse of himself. After all, we live in a world of reflecting surfaces— still water, shiny brass, stainless steel. I mean he never *looked*. He never stared into the mirror, asking why he was the way he was. He never seemed to care.
>
> Actually, he had looked in the mirror twice. Once, when he was younger, he looked in the mirror and saw someone different from those around him. He focused on his hair; it did not seem to be parted properly. He was not familiar with mirrors, so he reached out and brushed the mirror, trying again and again to straighten his part, but nothing changed. Maybe that failure planted a seed of distrust in mirrors. "Why look?" I can hear him say. "Nothing changes with the knowing."
>
> He looked in the mirror again when he was older and saw a wound, ragged and torn. He reached out and touched the mirror with skillful fingers to bind and sooth, but the wound remained ragged and the pain would not stop. I can hear him say, "Looking doesn't stop the pain. Nothing changes with the knowing."
>
> He never looked again.

Analysis

The seed for this story is the reality that what we see in the mirror cannot be touched—it is truth once removed. I wanted to explore the world of someone who did not see that distinction, someone who thought introspection was ineffective. I use this story to help people realize that things can change with the knowing. Looking, rightly understood, is of great benefit.

Example 15: Pictures

Situation

I was counseling a woman who was dealing with a number of difficult marital situations. As our weekly sessions progressed, I became uncomfortable with the sorts of things she was sharing. Here is the story I came up with:

> One afternoon, she carried her album into his office. The light was transparent, oblique with a shade of sunset and the implied promise of moonlight. She sat in the light, opened her book, and began to show him her pictures.
>
> The first picture she showed was a formal family portrait. She was seated surrounded by her daughters. Everyone was slightly stiff, carefully positioned to deflect the expected flash. He could see beyond the arrangement. Her daughters were young; so he knew that the neatly ironed dresses and the gleaming, braided hair were testimonies to her loving care. Her husband stood behind her, a bit apart. His tie matched his suit, and his suit blended in with the rest of the family, more evidence of a woman's touch. They were all smiling.
>
> He smiled back.
>
> The second picture she showed was more casual, almost relaxed. She was seated on a blanket under a spreading oak tree in a meadow near the crest of a hill. He could see her daughters in the distance, clustered by a fence beside a mare and two colts. On the blanket were empty bags of potato chips, crusts from peanut butter and jelly sandwiches, and empty boxes of apple juice. She was holding a book. He could not see the title, but he could tell by the binding that it was a serious book—no

gaudy romance—no frivolous novel. She seemed happy. Her legs were folded under, and her skirt was bunched up above her knees. The wind was gently pressing a cotton blouse against her torso and ruffling her hair. She looked direct, fresh, and somehow winsome.

He nodded and looked up from the album. She smiled enigmatically and turned the page.

The third picture was a pattern of black and white; actually it was a swirl of darkness and moonlight. At first, it was all reflecting curves and impenetrable shadow, but gradually his eyes adjusted and he realized it was a picture of her sitting alone on a stone bench in a garden beneath a vine trellis. She was half reclined on the bench, gentle white curves encased in an evening dress so black it gleamed in the darkness. One diamond sparkled around her neck, another one at her ear. The bars of the trellis and the entangling shadows of the vine obscured the expression on her face. All that could be seen was the tip of her tongue caught between the glimmer of moist lips and white teeth. She seemed to be waiting with the quiet stillness of a tiger.

He felt a vague apprehension and looked up again. She held up a hand as if to say, "Relax," and without a word she turned the page.

The fourth picture seemed out of order. It was old, the edge was cracked, and the colors had faded. Muted reds and washed-out yellows seeped into the underlying sepia. Centered against a small spare house was a little girl, angular, bony, intense. She was standing very straight wearing a plain cotton dress. On one knee was a soiled Band-Aid. Her socks drooped on worn leather shoes. Her hair was cropped just below her ears and she stared at the camera with an unsettling directness. He recognized her. In the little girl, he could see the woman she would become. As he looked at her, he could feel her stiffness, as if her spirit never quite fit her flesh. Her bony shoulders seemed braced for the burden she would someday carry. In her eyes he could see the shadows lurking like sharks in deep water. He noticed she was alone—all alone.

He spent a long time looking at that solitary child, and with a deep sigh he looked up into lonely eyes. She blinked once and turned the page.

A bed filled the image—a big, wide bed with red satin sheets. She was in the middle of the bed—naked—under the sheet but obviously naked. She lay on her back, bare arms over her head. Her eyes were closed; her lips were parted. She was not asleep, but she was still, very still—waiting.

His eyes darted back and forth over the picture, but there was nothing else to see, just the big, red bed and the waiting nakedness. He spoke into the stillness, "Why did you show me that?" He looked up to find her eyes fixed on his.

"Don't be afraid," she murmured. "They are only pictures." He sighed and wondered.

He realized, "I want to look so I must not look." With a deeper sigh he reached out and closed the book. Then he asked her to leave.

Analysis

Once, a client showed up for a session with some pictures. As she showed them to me, I realized she had chosen the pictures to convey a certain message. I realized that our sessions were just like that, different snapshots of her life. Eventually, I noticed that the trend of what she was showing me was dangerous.

This story is a warning that sometimes clients give us perilous information, and we need to know when to stop looking. Generally, we need to stop when we want to keep looking. I never shared this story with the woman who provoked it, but it did provide insight into what my response should be. I stopped looking and referred her to a professional counselor.

Example 16: More

Situation

Sometimes a wife wants a deeper relationship with her husband. Sometimes an adult child wants a deeper relationship with his father. Sometimes the person asks for more, only to discover the other party does not know how to respond. Here is the story:

> A man can live on a diet of vitamins—one oblong pill with plenty of water. Son knew this because he had done it for years. But one day, Son looked across the table at what his father had on his plate, and he wanted more.
>
> "I want more," Son said as he swallowed his vitamin. The emotion was blunt, and the "please" was belated.
>
> A small frown creased his father's forehead. The words were as familiar as waves on the beach. "We should be grateful for what we have.... When I was a boy I had much less and said nothing.... Remember, the starving children in China that do not even have vitamins." Still, in the silence between the waves, the echo whispered, "I want more."
>
> The next day, when Son sat down, there on his plate, beside the vitamin, was a color picture torn from a *Reader's Digest* magazine. It was a picture of a steaming Banquet chicken pot pie. The flaky tan crust was split invitingly, and he glimpsed orange carrots and chunks of white chicken submerged in thick yellow gravy.
>
> Son looked up. His father was watching—waiting. Son smiled and said, "I want more." Son could tell that his dissatisfaction was making his father dissatisfied. Son swallowed the vitamin with difficulty.
>
> The next day, when Son sat down, there on his plate,

beside the vitamin, was a vivid picture neatly trimmed from a smooth, glossy *National Geographic.* In the picture, on a bone china plate, dark brown gravy was spilling out of a volcano of mashed potatoes, coursing down to inundate tectonic folds of medium-rare roast beef. On the other side of the plate was an avalanche of bright yellow corn, glistening with butter. The picture was so vivid that Son could see the tendrils of steam rising from the food. His empty stomach growled.

He looked up with a determined smile of appreciation, but his father had heard the truth from his stomach. The words were redundant, but Son said them anyway: "I want more." Disappointment chased frustration in his father's eyes. The vitamin stuck in Son's throat.

On the third day, when Son sat down, there on his plate, beside the vitamin, was a stunning picture. It was a custom laser print, and the brilliant colors had a depth and presence that approached three-dimensional. In the picture was a glorious steak—thick, glistening, Grade AAA Prime—seared with the stripes of a red-hot grill. Beside this glorious steak was a magnificent baked potato, its crisp jacket split open exposing a creamy white interior with a generous pat of melting butter and an almost quivering dollop of sour cream. Two slices of roast apple added a splash of russet on the side.

Right in the middle of the picture was a small square that said, "Scratch here." Son reached out a tentative fingernail and slowly scratched. The smell of grilled steak filled his nostrils.

Son looked up, so overwhelmed that he could not smile. Tears welled up, and he brushed the vitamin off the table, crushed it with his foot and sobbed, "I want more." As he stumbled from the table, he couldn't help asking himself, "Why can't I be satisfied with what he has to give?"

Analysis

The story seed for this parable came from the stunning photographs of food in *Ladies Home Journal*. They looked so nourishing, but they were only the *appearance* of nourishment. Many relationships are like that. They appear to be nourishing but are actually shallow, almost two-dimensional. The parable is intended to provoke reflection on the depth of the relationships in our lives, with an encouragement to provide more than appearances.

Example 17: Invisible Blood

Situation

Often in ministry, someone will say something that will wound us deeply, and our response is paradoxical. We hide the pain but hope someone notices. Usually they do not. Here is the story:

> The room was full of friends. As I leaned on the counter, the party eddied around me. My friends smiled casually. A few caught my eye and nodded amiably. The soft murmur of conversation was like wheels on the interstate.
>
> My feet were far away—distant—disengaged. With a damp hand, I pressed the tail of my shirt into the wound. My breath was ragged ... my thoughts ... sluggish. I could feel the blood seeping stickily down my leg, puddling in my wing tip. All I could feel in my side was a deep ache and a pulsing throb nearer the surface. The room was getting dim in the corners, and shadows were collecting around the edges of the furniture. Each breath was an effort, and I could feel a gurgling rattle in my throat.
>
> I felt a distant bewilderment and the faint flutter of questions. Why didn't they notice my wound? Why didn't anyone move in my direction? Why were there no supporting arms around my shoulders? Why were no hurried fingers stabbing 9-1-1 into ever-present cell phones? Didn't anybody care? Was everybody going to quietly watch me bleed to death?

My head drooped. I blinked—once—twice, and then stared directly at my wound. With one last bitter smile it was suddenly obvious why no one helped—I was bleeding invisible blood. Who would believe that! I clenched my jaw, shut my mouth, and quietly slumped to the floor.

Analysis

Here the story seed came from a what-if question: "What if emotional wounds bled like physical wounds?" The emotional blood would be invisible. So the only way others would know we were wounded was if we told them. I told the story in first person to help the hearer gain even more distance from an intentionally grim description. The fact that I can tell the story is subtle evidence that I must have survived. I hoped the story would provoke the wounded to admit it and get help. I have used this story in counseling situations to encourage clients to acknowledge their wounding and receive help.

Example 18: Snakebit

Situation

Often, pornography is discussed as if it posed no real danger. As long as the sin can be kept secret, who is hurt? Of course, sin always manages to bite us. Here is the story:

It was late. The house was quiet. His family was asleep. Dan clicked off the TV, crossed the room, and quietly sat in front of his computer. When the AOL logo appeared, he logged in, and heard the muted, "You've got mail!" Most of it was routine, but one piece had a link with the promise of *Girls! Girls! Girls!* His heart beat a bit faster. His mouth went a bit dry. He took a deep breath and clicked on the link.

The screen darkened then resolved, showing the picture of a huge king cobra. Its hooded head swayed back and forth over thick, sinuous coils, and there was a menacing, guttural hiss.

Dan paused, puzzled—where were the girls? Then it was too late. The cobra struck out of the monitor and two-inch fangs sank deep into the soft part of Dan's neck, just above his heart. The neurotoxin burned, and his vision blurred, but through the haze Dan saw the snake retract into the monitor, saw the screen darken again and then resolve with *Girls! Girls! Girls!*

The poison burned as it pumped through his heart, and Dan slowly went numb.

Analysis

The story seed was the realization that Satan, the Great Serpent, strikes many men with the poison of computer pornography. What if the Serpent's strike were obvious? The story is intended to provoke insight into the secret poisoning that is going on when men look at pornography, as well as the usual result.

Example 19: Dancing

Situation

More and more often, pastors face the challenge of helping people recover from the devastating damage of childhood sexual abuse. Although professional counselors carry the therapeutic burden in most of these cases, a pastor can help provide a meta-narrative for the process and a glimmer of hope in the darkness. Here is the story:

Chapter 1: Broken

It was one of those quiet afternoons when the stillness is broken by small sounds—flies chasing each other from screen to screen, leaves fluttering in the languid breeze high in the kapok tree, the soft crinkle of magazine pages turning.

Sitting on the smooth, cool concrete floor was a little boy putting together a wooden puzzle—head bent in quiet concentration, legs crossed beneath him, pudgy fingers carefully putting each piece into place. In a chair nearby, his father was reading *Newsweek,* slowly, softly turning the pages. It was very quiet, very still—just a little boy sitting in a puddle of sunlight.

Footsteps—and a woman came around the corner carrying a large, black cast-iron frying pan. Without a word she stopped beside the little boy—her son—and swung the pan. There was a muffled snap, and the little boy sagged back as his leg flopped hopelessly oblique.

The little boy's eyes widened as he watched his mother, raise the pan again, then whirl and leave the room. A small whimper escaped, broke the silence, and died out as he looked up and saw his father watching. For an unblinking moment, his father looked at him, and then with the warning unspoken went back to his reading.

The sunlight moved behind a cloud, and the little boy lay quietly in a puddle of pain.

Chapter 2: Healing

There was no blood and no tears, so (apparently) no one noticed the little boy's broken limb splayed out at such an odd angle. Everyone made benign allowance for the boy's occasional awkwardness, and of course it was painful. At first, the pain was devastating, but eventually it subsided to merely awful, and finally to almost tolerable—a familiar agony. And his leg healed—crooked of course.

The little boy learned to walk—the aching, twisting, jarring torment deforming each limping step, but walking allowed him to get to where he needed to go. It was not graceful, but it was realistic.

Running was only a dream. The dream did not come often, but in the dream the little boy would be in a green and hilly land, maybe Scotland. He would be running down a valley, loose and free and joyous with a cool wind in his face. His lungs were deep and his eyes were clear, but his legs were the delight—strong, straight, agile, and tireless as they stretched in muscular rhythm to the beat of his heart. He would wake up . . . wistful. The little boy never dreamed of dancing.

Chapter 3: Broken Again

Years pass. The little boy is now a man with a ready smile, a practiced ease. The pain is hidden deep, like lava in a volcano. The years have taught the man to compensate for his limp: adjustments that veil the awkwardness. It would take a sharp eye to notice the deformity.

Then, one day, the man fell among thieves, and they stoned him and left him for dead. Someone found him and carried him to safety. When the man regained consciousness, a stranger spoke to him of his twisted leg. "It can be straight," the stranger said. "How?" the man sighed without hope. A sadness shadowed the stranger's eyes. "It can be straight, but only through more pain. You will have to show me your leg, let me touch it, and—" the stranger paused and took a deeper breath. "And, it will need to be broken again so it can heal properly."

"Why should I do that?" Despair colored the man's voice, but he spoke with dispirited confidence. "The wound is an ancient one, and I am used to the pain. Nothing would be different."

The stranger smiled a solemn smile and made this promise:

> Everything will be different.
> This time you will not be alone.
> I will be there.
> I will care.

The man wavered. His faith was small and the pain was large, but as he looked into the eyes of the stranger again, he saw the glint of tears, deep and far away, like water at the bottom of a well.

Slowly, the man uncovered his crippled leg. The stranger did not look away, and the tears welled up and spilled over as the stranger gripped the man's leg with firm yet gentle hands. There was another muffled snap and the agony began again.

Chapter 4: Healing

A long time later—rivers of tears, oceans of despair, moonless nights, sunless days, summers without rain, winters without fire—the leg began to heal. The stranger patiently helped the man to walk, reminding him not to limp: "No need! No need!" And the man walked.

The stranger eventually provoked the man to run, and although it was never as good as in the dream, the man found the impossible was only difficult. And he ran.

Finally, one sweet day, the stranger said, "Tonight, you dance!" And that night, under brilliant stars, the music played. And with only the memory of a limp, the man began to dance.

Analysis

The seed for this story came from a therapist friend. This story is intended to provide understanding and hope during a long and very difficult healing process. I have shared this on several occasions, changing the gender of the protagonist as needed, and it has always been helpful. When therapy is over and I ask my clients which stories they remember, they almost always mention this one.

Example 20: Jump!
Situation

Every pastor I know has endured at least one season of church conflict. One of mine began when the governing board began to question my leadership. I was trying hard, but their systematic lack of support rendered me more and more ineffective. That frustrating situation provoked this story:

> They had a certified frog. They had checked, and the frog had all the appropriate tattoos. One front leg read, *Encouragement;* the other, *Support.* One powerful back leg read, *Resources;* the other, *Staff.* A fine, certified frog.
>
> One day they decided to see how far the frog could jump. They chalked a line on the floor, put the frog on the line and shouted, "Jump!" Startled, the frog leaped a long and lovely leap. "Wonderful!" they exulted, and when they measured, the frog had jumped four feet. The record read, "with four feet—4 feet."
>
> "I wonder what would happen . . ." and with that they decided to experiment. They snipped off the leg that read, *Encouragement.*
>
> They put the frog on the floor again and shouted, "Jump!" The frog paused a moment to center and then sprang forward. "Not bad, but not as good as before" was the general consensus, and the record read, "with three feet—3 feet."
>
> Next they snipped off *Support.* Without *Encouragement* or *Support,* the frog wavered a bit trying to find its balance, but when they shouted, "Jump!" it jumped. The landing was not elegant. With no front legs, it was sort of a tumbling flop of a landing, but some distance was covered. "Not so good" was the verdict, and the record read, "with two feet—2 feet."
>
> Next they snipped off a back leg—no more *Resources.* This time, when they put the frog on the line, it was obvious the frog was in distress. It wobbled desperately, trying to steady itself on only one foot. There was a short silence, and then in unison they shouted, "Jump!" The frog stiffened and with a brief spasm it made an awkward hop

down the floor. "That was pathetic," the team concluded with disappointment. Their disappointment continued as they recorded, "with one foot—1 foot."

"One more time," they concluded and snipped off the final leg. This time when the frog was put on the line he seemed limp and resigned. This time when they shouted, "Jump!" the frog did not move. Startled, they shouted a bit louder, "Jump!" The frog did not move. This irritated them, so they gathered around the frog and leaned in close. "Jump!" they shouted. "Jump! Jump! Jump!" They were screaming now, but the frog did not move.

"We have a problem," they concluded. They reviewed the record. The trend was clear, it did not take long to come to the only reasonable conclusion—the problem was the frog. The frog would not jump.

That conclusion prompted a bit more discussion about motive. Was the frog suddenly disobedient or simply un-cooperative? Maybe it was a bad frog from the beginning. They finally had to admit that the frog's motive was un-clear. In the interest of charity, they should simply record the facts. The clerk was instructed to make one last entry: "No legs: frog pretends to be deaf."

There was only one thing left to say, and someone said it as the lights went out. "We need a new frog."

Analysis

The story seed for this parable came from an Aggie joke I heard in Texas. The twist was to imagine myself as the frog. With this story, I hoped to make the point that if a governing board system-atically snips away everything a leader needs to be successful, they should not be surprised when the leader performs poorly. I never shared this story with my board. By the time I came up with it, all my legs were gone. I have shared it with several other pastors who I sensed were in similar situations, and it always provokes a rueful laugh.

Looking Back

These examples demonstrate that original ministry stories can be created to respond to a variety of situations. None of mine are as elegant as the ones that Jesus told, but they work and they help. I hope they provoke you to realize that you could do the same. You are surrounded with story seeds that could be planted, and with a little care, they will produce an abundant crop of your own original ministry stories, which will enrich your life and nourish your ministry. In the next chapter, I will offer some suggestions on how you can create an environment that encourages storymaking.

CHAPTER EIGHT

How to Encourage Stories

The real voyage of discovery consists not in seeking new lands but in having new eyes.

—MARCEL PROUST

STORIES ARE SO COMPELLING, RELATIONAL, and effective that it is to our benefit to create an environment in which storymaking is encouraged and flourishes. In this final chapter, I want to encourage you to create that sort of environment where you minister or work.

Create a Storymaking Environment

Three elements produce a healthy storymaking environment. Each element is important, and so is the sequence. We create this healthy environment when we listen well, respond with stories, and treat others with respect.

Listen Well

Effective storymaking begins with careful listening. Del Chinchen, a missionary educator working in a storytelling culture in Africa, offers this practical advice:

> There is a time to listen and an appropriate time to talk.
> It is all in the timing. Counsel, if not at the right time and
> in the right context, could do more harm than good. A
> word of wisdom is expected, sometimes in the form of a
> proverb (softening the blow of the advice), but only after
> careful listening.[1]

A good parable offered at the wrong time is a waste of effort.

Careful listening not only provides clues as to the appropriate time to offer a story, but it can also help you decide what story to tell. If you decide to make up a story on the spot, careful listening will give you insight into what sort of characters and situations might be most effective. Jesus probably listened long and hard before he chose to make a Samaritan the hero of his story about loving neighbors. Perhaps in the Old West the hero of the story would have been an Oglala Sioux. Perhaps in England, the hero would be Irish. Perhaps in the Middle East, the hero would be a Palestinian. Careful listening will enhance your effectiveness.

Respond with Stories

Careful listening often leads to a storytelling opportunity. When I listen to your story, you are inclined to listen to mine. We help create a storytelling environment when we recognize the dynamic, seize the opportunity, and tell a story. Terry Quong and Allan Walker, researchers writing for the educational community, observe, "Effective leaders are good listeners who actively encourage storytelling, and retelling, to bring about change."[2] A leader actively encourages storytelling primarily by telling stories whenever an opportunity presents itself. When the leader faces a communication opportunity and responds with a story, he or

---

1. Del Chinchen, "African Psychology: Established Counseling Techniques and Practices," *Evangelical Missions Quarterly* 40, no. 1 (2004): 59.
2. Terry Quong and Allan Walker, *Dealing with Bullying: Using Stories to Bring About Change* (Online Conference Management, 2000, accessed October 18 2004); available from http://www.apapdc.edu.au/archive/aspa/conference2000/papers/art_2_10.htm.

she models the desired behavior, and that example will eventually encourage others to respond with stories.

In my experience, people begin to respond with stories in four identifiable stages:

1. They listen to my stories. Often there is a nonverbal response of mild surprise and careful attention.
2. They begin to expect a story from me. They will often verbalize an anticipatory response like, "I suppose you have a story for that?" or "Does that remind you of a story?"
3. They begin to use stories in conversations with me. "I know you like stories, so let me explain it like this. This situation is like . . ."
4. They begin using stories in their conversations with others.

When our listeners begin using stories of their own, with others, we can be sure that our efforts to create a supportive environment are beginning to succeed.

Be Respectful

The third aspect of a healthy storymaking environment is respect for the listener. Stories are inherently respectful, because they invite a response but do not coerce one. Thomas Boomershine, a preacher and educator, makes the point:

> The most critical element in sharing these stories is to protect the freedom of the listener. Biblical stories are not designed to persuade or to manipulate a listener into agreement. To be sure, there are appeals, and the stories are structured to invite a response. But the freedom of the listener to respond in a variety of ways is built into the stories.[3]

---

3. Thomas E. Boomershine, *Story Journey: An Invitation to the Gospel as Storytelling* (Nashville: Abingdon, 1988), 52.

Marshall Shelley makes a similar point in his advice about telling stories to children:

> Stories can teach important lessons about life. Yet, because of the power of this face-to-face encounter, they should not become sledgehammers used to pound truth into ignorant and ornery urchins. Instead, stories should be seeds that implant concepts, attitudes, values, and character traits.[4]

Stories are very powerful and should be used in a respectful way. When we listen carefully, and respond with a story regularly and respectfully, we create an environment in which stories and storytelling flourish.

Looking Back

I suppose if we were talking you might say, "This book was helpful. I can see that stories are powerful. I can think of situations where a ministry story would really help, but I am not sure I can do this. I do not know where I would start." If you said that, I would say this:

> My friend, that is a normal feeling but a temporary one. It is like feeling out of breath when you start running. If you continue, you will get your second wind. If you persist in your desire to tell a story, you will get a second wind of inspiration.

Nancy Mellon, a veteran storyteller, put it like this, "You, like every human being, are a storyteller by birthright. You are born with an endless supply of personal and universal themes. It is important to open yourself to receive the vast wealth of imagery that lives within you."[5] In her effusive way, she makes a good point:

---

4. Marshall Shelley, *Telling Stories to Children* (Batavia, IL: Lion, 1990), 103–4.
5. Nancy Mellon, *Storytelling and the Art of Imagination* (Cambridge, MA: Yellow Moon, 1992), 8.

there are story seeds everywhere. If you desire to tell stories, you will soon start to see viable seeds in the things you read, commercials on TV, radio interviews, pet antics—ideas really are everywhere. The key to seeing these seeds is your desire to tell a story. Your desire will create an internal paradigm shift, and everything will be the same but different.

I encourage you to stimulate that desire. Tell more stories. Create some of your own ministry stories. Let the Holy Spirit flow through you the way he did through our Lord Jesus Christ to the glory of God the Father.

Bibliography

Allender, Dan B. *The Healing Path.* Colorado Springs: Waterbrook, 1999.

———. "The Wounded Heart." Speech, Covenant Seminary, St. Louis, MO, 1998.

Ameis, Jerry A. "Stories Invite Children to Solve Mathematical Problems." *Teaching Children Mathematics* 8, no. 5 (January 2002): 260–64.

Anderson, Leith. *Leadership That Works.* Grand Rapids: Bethany, 1999.

Askham, J. "Telling Stories." *Sociological Review* 30, no. 4 (1982): 555–74.

Bailey, Kenneth E. *Finding the Lost: Cultural Keys to Luke 15.* St. Louis: Concordia, 1992.

Barna, George. *A Fish Out of Water.* Nashville: Integrity, 2002.

Blackaby, Henry T., and Richard Blackaby. *Spiritual Leadership: Moving People on to God's Agenda.* Nashville: Broadman & Holman, 2001.

Boomershine, Thomas E. *Story Journey: An Invitation to the Gospel as Storytelling.* Nashville: Abingdon, 1988.

Borden, Paul. "Is There Really One Big Idea in That Story?" In *The Big Idea of Biblical Preaching,* ed. Keith Willhite and Scott M. Gibson, 67–80. Grand Rapids: Baker, 1998.

Borsch, Frederick Houk. *Many Things in Parables: Extravagant Stories of New Community.* Philadelphia: Fortress, 1988.

Bradt, Kevin M. *Story as a Way of Knowing.* Kansas City, MO: Sheed & Ward, 1997.

Bruner, Jerome. *Acts of Meaning.* Cambridge, MA: Harvard, 1990.

Buckler, Sheldon A., and Karen Anne Zien. "The Spirituality of Innovation: Learning from Stories." *Journal of Product Innovation Management* 13 (1996): 391–405.

Chinchen, Del. "African Psychology: Established Counseling Techniques and Practices." *Evangelical Missions Quarterly* 40, no. 1 (2004): 54–59.

Combs, Martha, and John D. Beach. "Stories and Storytelling: Personalizing the Social Studies." *The Reading Teacher* 47, no. 6 (1994): 464–71.

Crossan, John Dominic. *In Parables: The Challenge of the Historical Jesus.* New York: Harper & Row, 1973.

Dawes, Milton. "Science, Religion and God: My Story." *ETC: A Review of General Semantics* 57, no. 2 (2000): 147–60.

Dent, Don. "Making It Stick." *Evangelical Missions Quarterly* 40, no. 2 (2004): 152–58.

Durrance, Bonnie. "Stories at Work." *Training and Development* 51, no. 2 (1997): 25–30.

Evans, Craig A. "Parables in Early Judaism." In *The Challenge of Jesus' Parables,* ed. Richard N. Longenecker, 51–75. Grand Rapids: Eerdmans, 2000.

Galli, Mark, and Craig Brian Larson. *Preaching That Connects.* Grand Rapids: Zondervan, 1994.

George, Timothy. "Is Christ Divided?" *Christianity Today,* July 2005, 30–33.

Gowler, David B. *What Are They Saying About the Parables?* Mahwah, NJ: Paulist, 2000.

Hultgren, Arland J. *The Parables of Jesus: A Commentary.* Grand Rapids: Eerdmans, 2000.

Hybels, Bill. *Courageous Leadership.* Grand Rapids: Zondervan, 2002.

Jacks, G. Robert. *Just Say the Word: Writing for the Ear.* Grand Rapids: Eerdmans, 1996.

Jeremias, Joachim. *The Parables of Jesus.* 2d rev. ed. Upper Saddle River, NJ: Prentice Hall, 1972.

Kingsolver, Barbara. *The Poisonwood Bible.* New York: HarperCollins, 1998.

Lewis, C. S. *Of Other Worlds.* New York: Harvest, 1966.

McArthur, Harvey K., and Robert M. Johnston. *They Also Taught in Parables.* Grand Rapids: Zondervan, 1990.

McManus, Erwin Raphael. *An Unstoppable Force: Daring to Become the Church God Had in Mind.* Loveland, CO: Group, 2001.

Mellon, Nancy. *Storytelling and the Art of Imagination.* Cambridge, MA: Yellow Moon, 1992.

Misal, Bello Melton. "An Interpretation of the Agricultural Parables of the Kingdom in Matthew 13:1–31 in an African Cultural Background." Th.M. thesis, Biola University, 1990.

Peterson, James. "Once Upon a Time." *Paths of Learning,* no. 14 (2002): 33–39.

Powell, Mark A. *What Is Narrative Criticism?* Minneapolis, MN: Fortress, 1990.

Powers, Amy. "Mommy's Song." Used by permission.

Quong, Terry, and Allan Walker. *Dealing with Bullying: Using Stories to Bring About Change.* Online Conference Management, 2000, accessed 18 October 2004; available from http://www.apapdc.edu.au/archive/aspa/conference2000/papers/art_2_10.htm.

"Quotable Quotes." *Reader's Digest,* November 2002, 73.

Robinson, Haddon W. *Biblical Preaching.* 2d ed. Grand Rapids: Baker, 2001.

Shaw, Susan M. *Storytelling in Religious Education.* Birmingham, AL: Religious Education Press, 1999.

Shelley, Marshall. *Telling Stories to Children.* Batavia, IL: Lion, 1990.

Silver, David. "Songs and Storytelling: Bringing Health Messages to Life in Uganda." *Education for Health: Change in Learning and Practice* 14, no. 1 (2001): 51–61.

Steffen, Tom A. "Congregational Character: From Stories to Story." *Journal of the American Society for Church Growth* 11, no. 2 (2000): 17–31.

————. *Reconnecting God's Story to Ministry: Crosscultural Storytelling at Home and Abroad.* La Habra, CA: Center for Organizational and Ministry Development, 1996.

————. "Rethinking the Role of Narrative in Mission Training." *Occasional Bulletin of the Evangelical Missiological Society* 9, no. 3 (1997): 1–6.

Stein, Robert H. "The Genre of the Parables." In *The Challenge of Jesus' Parables,* ed. Richard N. Longenecker, 30–50. Grand Rapids: Eerdmans, 2000.

————. *An Introduction to the Parables of Jesus.* Philadelphia: Westminster, 1981.

Thomson, Clarence. *Parables and the Enneagram.* Portland, OR: Metamorphous, 1996.

Tirrell, Lynne. "Storytelling and Moral Agency." *Journal of Aesthetics and Art Criticism* 48, no. 2 (1990): 115–27.

Von Baeyer, Hans Christian. "Tangled Tales." *Sciences* 41, no. 2 (2001): 14–18.

Walsh, John. *The Art of Storytelling: Easy Steps to Presenting an Unforgettable Story.* Chicago: Moody, 2003.

Young, Brad H. *Jesus and His Jewish Parables: Rediscovering the Roots of Jesus' Teaching.* Mahwah, NJ: Paulist, 1989.

Title Index

Name	Storymaker
Stories and Songs	James Peterson 10
Flawed Diamond	Clarence Thomson 20–21
Gorilla Hunters	Bello Misal. 22–23
The Supportive Small Group	Bill Hybels 38–39
The Wise Sheep Dogs	Rabbis. 70
The Judge, the Dog, and the Moon	*Bits and Pieces* 71
Fox and Fish	R. Akiba. 72–73
Parish Poker	Leith Anderson 73–76
Fire, Prayer and Place	Hasidim 76–77
Mommy's Song	Amy Powers. 78–79
Faux Parable—The Rich Young Ruler	George Barna. 84
Two Sons	D. Bruce Seymour. 84–87
Not Your Wool	D. Bruce Seymour. 92–93
All You See	D. Bruce Seymour. 93–94
The Tree	D. Bruce Seymour. 94–95
Can't Won't Jane	D. Bruce Seymour. 96–97
My Favorites	D. Bruce Seymour. 97–98
Options	D. Bruce Seymour. 98–99

Good Possums   D. Bruce Seymour. 100–102
It's All Good   D. Bruce Seymour. 102–3
The Gift   D. Bruce Seymour. 103–4
Soup   D. Bruce Seymour. 104–6
Guess Who   D. Bruce Seymour. 106–7
Dark Pieces   D. Bruce Seymour. 107–9
Collateral Damage   D. Bruce Seymour. 109–10
Reflections   D. Bruce Seymour. 111–12
Pictures   D. Bruce Seymour. 112–15
More   D. Bruce Seymour. 115–17
Invisible Blood   D. Bruce Seymour. 117–18
Snakebit   D. Bruce Seymour. 118–19
Dancing   D. Bruce Seymour. 119–22
Jump!   D. Bruce Seymour. 123–25

Topical Index

If You Need a Story About . . .	Consider Using . . .
Abuse	Dark Pieces 107–9
	Collateral Damage 109–10
	Dancing 119–22
Arriving late	Can't Won't Jane 96–97
Boundaries	Pictures 112–15
Choruses	My Favorites 97–98
Church discipline	Options 98–99
Compliments	Guess Who. 106–7
Conflict	Jump! 123–25
Counseling	Reflections 111–12
	Pictures 112–15
	Dancing 119–22
Criticism	Invisible Blood 117–18
Dying church	The Tree. 94–95
Encouragement	Guess Who. 106–7
Financial assistance	All You See. 93–94
Governing board	Jump! 123–25

History   Dark Pieces 107–9
Hymns   My Favorites 97–98
Introspection   Reflections 111–12
Judgment   The Tree 94–95
Leadership Style   Good Possums 100–102
Missionaries   Not Your Wool 92–93
                     All You See 93–94
Music   My Favorites 97–98
Offended   My Favorites 97–98
                     Soup 104–6
Parents   Collateral Damage 109–10
Participation   Not Your Wool 92–93
                     It's All Good 102–3
Passivity   Good Possums 100–102
Pastoral Care   Options 98–99
Pornography   Snakebit 118–19
Potty runs   Can't Won't Jane 96–97
Pyramid sales   All You See 93–94
Relationship   More 115–17
Self-image   Guess Who 106–7
Sin   Snakebit 118–19
Spiritual gifts   The Gift 103–4
Support   All You See 93–94
                     Jump! 123–25
Trouble   Options 98–99
                     Dark Pieces 107–9
Wounds   Invisible Blood 117–18

A Definitive Resource for Preachers

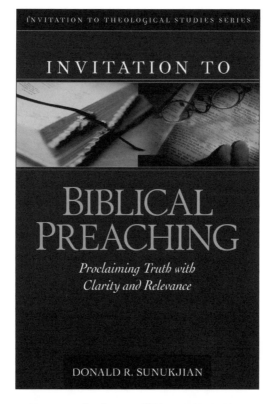

384 pages • hardcover • ISBN 978-0-8254-3666-6

Invitation to Biblical Preaching takes the reader step-by-step through the entire process of biblical preaching—from biblical study to planning to delivery. Both current pastors and those training for the pulpit will especially appreciate the book's original content, profuse examples, and clear instruction. Two complete sermons (one from the Old Testament and one from the New Testament) reinforce the text's principles.

"Will help any pastor to preach with variety."

—Scott M. Gibson,
AUTHOR OF *Preaching the Old Testament*

240 pages • paperback • ISBN 978-0-8254-2019-1

Preaching with Variety reveals how pastors can preach creatively by borrowing the dynamics of six genres or forms found in the Bible. Each chapter includes practical "Try this" suggestions and ends with a quick checklist for preachers to consider when preaching from each of the six genres. Readers will learn how to expand their repertoire of creative, interesting, and relevant sermons.

A Must-Have Resource for Every Pastor and Worship Leader

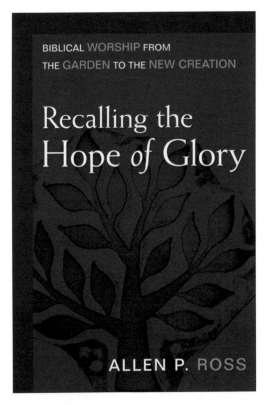

BIBLICAL WORSHIP FROM THE GARDEN TO THE NEW CREATION

Recalling the Hope of Glory

ALLEN P. ROSS

592 pages • hardcover • ISBN 978-0-8254-3578-2

Neither technical, simplistic, nor specific to one denomination, *Recalling the Hope of Glory* is an inductive study of worship throughout the entire Bible. Noted commentator Allen P. Ross (*Holiness to the Lord*) also considers the historical development of worship from the religious world in antiquity and worship in the early church to modern traditions and liturgy.